Classic Rovers

# Classic Rovers
## 1934-1986

A collector's guide
by James Taylor

MOTOR RACING PUBLICATIONS LTD
Unit 6, The Pilton Estate, 46 Pitlake, Croydon CRO 3RY, England


First published 1983
Reprinted 1989
2nd edition 1996

**British Library Cataloguing in Publication Data**

Taylor, James, 1950-
    Classic Rovers, 1945-1986 : a collector's guide. – 2nd ed.
    1. Rover automobile – History  2. Rover automobile –
    Collectors and collecting
    I. Title
    629.2'222

ISBN 1-899870-07-5


Printed in Great Britain by
The Amadeus Press Ltd
Huddersfield, West Yorkshire

# Contents

# Introduction

Interest in the Rovers built during the company's Solihull period has grown to a quite astonishing degree since I prepared the first edition of this book in 1983. Even the SD1 models – which were then still in production and widely scorned for the poor build quality which afflicted so many early examples – have become accepted as objects of enthusiast interest, and now have their own thriving owners' club. As stocks of the original book (reprinted in 1989) ran low and it was clear that a further reprint would be needed, I discussed the way forward with my publishers at MRP. We agreed that we should include the SD1 models in the new edition, and we also reluctantly agreed that the chapters on the cars of the 1930s would have to be omitted in order to make room. So this book is entitled *The Classic Rovers, 1945-1986*, whereas its predecessor was *The Classic Rovers, 1934-1977*.

We hope our decision to focus on the cars of the Solihull period does not upset too many Rover devotees. I would certainly argue that the Solihull period is a clearly-defined era of Rover history, a period when the company's products came from the same core team of designers and engineers. By the time the last SD1 was built in 1986, things had changed irrevocably. Rover car assembly had moved out of Solihull (at the end of 1981) to make room for expanded Land-Rover and Range Rover production, the key members of the old design team had gone, and the new Rovers were already envisaged as joint products with the Japanese Honda company – indeed, one of them had been in production since 1984. It was a sad end for a proud company, but Rover enthusiasts can take comfort in two facts: firstly, that the Rover name was so highly regarded that it came to be used for the whole of what had once been British Leyland after 1986; and secondly, that the Rover tradition lives on at Solihull in the shape of the Land Rover and its relatives.

In the earlier versions of this book, I argued that the revived prewar Rovers which entered production at Solihull late in 1945 must have been known internally as P1s, and that the P2 was an interim development of these which was abandoned in favour of the 1948 production P3. A decade and a half of research has still failed to find any reference to a P1 in the Rover archives, or any Rover engineer who remembered the name being used. What it has done, however, is to show that P2 was actually the name used for the revived prewar cars. Several Rover engineers have also adamantly insisted that the 'P' prefix stood for 'Postwar'. The number '1' appears to have been allocated to the

M-type (often referred to as the M1), the miniature Rover which was abandoned at the prototype stage; the number '2' was then logically allocated to the next project, which was the one to revive the prewar models.

P2 was, of course, followed by P3, P4, P5 and P6. The P7 did not go beyond the prototype stage, P8 was cancelled at the last minute and P9 was also abandoned. The P10 eventually became SD1 (Specialist Division no.1). These, then, are the cars covered in this book – and for completeness there are also brief details of the aborted projects from Rover's Solihull period.

Woodcote, Oxfordshire, August 1996
JAMES L. TAYLOR

# Acknowledgements

It is simply not possible to list all the people who have provided information which eventually ended up in this book. However, I must record my very special thanks to the former Rover employees who have willingly raked through their memories to help me try to get the facts right. I hope I have not misrepresented what they have said to me during a period of research which is now approaching 20 years.

J.L.T.

This 1947 16hp Sports Saloon shows off the lines of the immediate postwar models. They were the same as the prewar cars but for minor details, and were known as P2 models.

Last of the Classic Rovers. The early 2000 looked very much the poor relative of the range with its plastic wheel trims. The bumpers lacked the bright trim found on more expensive models, and there was no front spoiler. The enlarged rear window of the facelifted cars is clearly visible here.

# CHAPTER 1

# One of Britain's Fine Cars

## The revived prewar models, 1946–1947

**10hp, 12hp, 14hp and 16hp (1946-1947)**
The cars whose story is told in this book were all built at Rover's Solihull factory, except for a few built overseas from knock-down kits and the final SD1s which were assembled at Cowley. Solihull was the centre of Rover operations for 36 years, and it still is the home of the Land-Rover which the company introduced in 1948 when it was desperate for a new product to sell abroad.

However, Rover's home before the 1939-1945 war was not in Solihull but in Coventry. It was there that the brothers Maurice and Spencer Wilks, Chief Engineer and Managing Director respectively, completely turned around the fortunes of a company which had been on its knees at the end of the 1920s. Spencer Wilks was the driving force behind a new policy which put quality before quantity, and his younger brother designed the new range of cars which reached the showrooms in the autumn of 1933.

These cars had very distinctive characteristics of discreet good looks, above-average performance and first-rate build quality which gave them a strong appeal to the professional middle classes. They established an image for Rover which still endures today, despite the damage which early examples of the SD1 did to it in the late 1970s. Their sales success was also immediate. Rover's modest profit of £7,511 for 1932 – itself a vast improvement on the £80,000 loss recorded in 1931 – had grown into a net profit of £156,282 by 1936, the year when a second generation of Wilks Rovers was introduced to replace the first.

The year 1936 was also notable for the fact that Rover was chosen by the British Government as one of several established motor manufacturers who were to manage the new 'shadow factories'. These factories were then being planned to duplicate or 'shadow' the aircraft factories, in case their additional production capacity was needed in wartime. By 1936, although the Government was loath to admit it, war with Hitler's Germany was looking increasingly inevitable, and the Air Ministry wanted to ensure that it was well prepared for the air war which it already suspected might be a decisive element in any future hostilities. The first Rover-managed 'shadow' factory was erected at Acocks Green in 1936-37, and a second and much larger one was built on a greenfield site at Solihull in 1939-40.

Rover's own factory in Coventry's Helen Street was bombed into ruins by the Luftwaffe on November 14, 1940, and so when the war ended and private car production was once again permitted by the Government, the Rover Company moved lock, stock and barrel into the Solihull 'shadow' factory. Helen Street was patched up and sold, and the Company's designers settled down to the awesome task of catching up on three years' worth of advances in automotive engineering from across the Atlantic. In the meantime, it was vital to get production started again and to have cars in the showrooms. There were obviously no new models ready (although the Rover designers were working on a new small car called the M-type, which never made it into production), and so Spencer Wilks instructed that the prewar models should go back into production. These cars

This shot of Rover's entries for the 1937 RAC Rally makes an interesting comparison between the old and the new models. Differences are most apparent in the shape of the front wings. The Tourer, of course, is a Speed model with the special headlamp and horn arrangement and the centre-lock wire wheels. The 1937 model alongside is a six-light Saloon.

differed only slightly from their 1936-40 counterparts, but they were now known at Solihull as the P2 range. The 'P' stood for postwar, and the '2' probably indicated the second design, the little M-type being the first.

Materials shortages were the order of the day, and the economic climate favoured small cars rather than large ones. So the prewar range did not go back into production in its entirety. The largest-engined car – the 2,512cc 20hp model – was dropped from the range and Rover announced only the 10hp, 12hp, 14hp and 16hp models for the 1946 season. The gearbox was also redesigned, and the P2 Rovers were made available for the first time with left-hand drive as a consequence of the Government's demand for exports. Before the war, Rover had never taken overseas markets at all seriously, and its only concession in that direction had been the fitting of larger wheels and tyres to 'Colonial' models in the 1930s!

Even so, production was slow to get under way in the new factory. The first postwar Rovers to be built were in fact two 10hp models which left Solihull in December 1945, some two months before the official opening of the factory on February 2, 1946 by Sir Stafford Cripps, then President of the Board of Trade. Black paint and brown upholstery were the only colours supplied at first, and left-hand-drive cars also took their time to filter through. At first the only left-hand-drive models were 16hp Saloons, although the 16hp

Sports Saloon and 10hp Saloon followed for the 1947 season.

Rover advertised the P2 models with the patriotic slogan, "One of Britain's Fine Cars", but not surprisingly made very few changes to the specification during their two seasons of production. Solihull's efforts were directed towards designing entirely new models in preference to facelifting the old. In the event, P2 production lasted some six months longer than planned when the Land-Rover held up introduction of the replacement models in 1947. The last P2s left the production lines before Christmas 1947, after which retooling began for the production of the P3 models for introduction in February 1948.

**Chassis and engines**
The basic design of the P2 chassis dated back to the 1934 models introduced in the autumn of 1933, and had been drawn up by Maurice Wilks. Its channel-section side-members swept under the rear axle, and were braced by a number of pressed crossmembers. However, the frame was not particularly stiff in torsion, and to damp out front end shimmy over bumps, a Wilmot-Breeden harmonic stabilizer was fitted behind the front bumper. This was actually a very long transverse leaf spring with heavy bob-weights attached to its ends and concealed inside the end rolls of the bumper.

The live rear and beam front axles were both sprung by

All finishing work was carried out by hand. Here, six-light bodyshells are being rubbed down prior to the application of the first colour coat. These are postwar models, photographed at Solihull in 1946.

semi-elliptic leaf springs with hydraulic piston-type dampers. All models except the 10hp also had anti-roll bars front and rear. Brakes were a Girling rod-operated type, and there was a Luvax-Bijur centralized chassis lubrication system which was intended to reduce maintenance by delivering a shot of lubrication to 23 points on the chassis when a hand-plunger inside the car was pressed. In practice, however, the pipes tended to become clogged unless as much maintenance was given to the automatic lubrication system as would otherwise have been given to the chassis!

Four different engines were on offer, the 10hp and 12hp types having four cylinders and the 14hp and 16hp having six. All of them were derived from a single overhead-valve design drawn up for the first-generation Wilks Rovers by Maurice Wilks and his assistant Robert Boyle, and all of them shared the same 100mm stroke. The 10hp had a swept volume of 1,389cc, the 12hp had 1,496cc, the 14hp had 1,901cc (and was actually rated by the RAC as a 15hp) and the 16hp had 2,147cc. Performance in every case was respectable rather than dazzling, aided by the positive short-

throw change action of the four-speed gearbox which had synchromesh on third and top gears. All models were also fitted with the traditional Rover freewheel, which was controlled from the dashboard and allowed clutchless gearchanges as well as a drop in engine revs (to the benefit of both durability and fuel consumption) when the car was coasting.

**Bodies**

The bodies of the P2 models had steel panels on ash frames and were built at Solihull. They had been designed by Maurice Wilks in conjunction with Harry Loker, and had deliberately echoed elements of the elegant 1933 Hastings Coupe design drawn up by Carbodies of Coventry as an option for the six-cylinder chassis of the time. Yet where the Carbodies design had just two doors, Rover's had four. Two varieties were available: the six-light Saloon on all variants and the slightly lower and more rakish four-light Sports Saloon on the 12hp, 14hp and 16hp only. Both bodies clearly came from the same family, with their helmet-shaped front wings, gently raked windscreens and a circular impression on the drop-down lid of the squarish box-boot which betrayed the position of the spare wheel. Sliding roofs were still *de rigueur* in this class of car, and both Saloons and Sports Saloons had them.

Saloon models carried a pass lamp on their nearside dumb-irons and a chromed horn on their offisde dumb-irons, but the Sports Saloons had a chromed trumpet-horn on each dumb-iron and a triangular support bar between them which carried the pass lamp. Bonnet sides were plain on the 10hp, 12hp and 14hp models, while the 16hp had two hinged ventilator flaps in each side. Just to confuse the issue, however, 250 16hp Saloons and 50 16hp Sports Saloons built in 1947 had plain bonnet sides, probably because stocks of these bonnets were being used up as production drew to an end.

These Rover saloons offered their occupants a remarkable degree of comfort. All seats were located within the wheelbase, and yet there was ample room for the legs of rear seat passengers, who were also provided with

A 1938 14hp six-light Saloon, seen in 1981. Bonnet sides are plain, unlike those of the 1937 model. The 'box boot' was characteristic of both the four-light and six-light bodies.

By 1947, when this 16hp Sports Saloon was built, Easyclean disc wheels were standard. The photographer was Alan Milstead.

12

Dashboard of a 1947 model. The large turnwheel control operated the freewheel, and the winder in the centre of the facia rail opened the windscreen. The two knobs below this worked the windscreen wipers; the passenger-side arm could be switched out when not required. Note also the under-dash tool tray, just visible on the left, and the footwell air vent. The badge at the base of the instrument panel reads 'Coachwork by Rover'; P3 and later bodies were built by Pressed Steel.

substantial armrests. Upholstery was, of course, always in pleated leather. A rear window blind could be pulled up by a cord reaching to the driver's position, and Saloon bodies had a parcels net in the roof to keep bulky items from under the passengers' feet. The instruments were neatly laid out in the centre of the wooden dashboard which was dominated by a huge spring-spoke steering wheel, and a tool kit was fitted in a sliding tray under the passenger's side of the dashboard. Buyers of 1946 models had to make do without a heater, but the final year's production from January 1947 had Clayton-Dewandre heater-demisters as standard. These last cars also had a modified facia which allowed an extra-cost radio to be installed under the centre, and a thermostatically-controlled choke warning light took the place of the trafficator telltale on the dash.

Despite the postwar restrictions and conditions, Rover did manage to get a third body style into production. This was an open Tourer, introduced on the 12hp chassis probably in the early spring of 1947 and theoretically for export only. However, as all the Tourer bodies were fitted to right-hand-drive chassis, a few not surprisingly found their way on to the home market! A rumour persists that some Tourer bodies were fitted to 10hp chassis, although neither records nor actual cars have ever been found to substantiate this.

The Tourer bodies shared almost none of the lines of the contemporary closed bodies, principally because Maurice Wilks and Harry Loker had based them on the body of a 1934 Tourer which Rover had bought back for the purpose because the original drawings had been lost during the war. However, the new Tourer was not a slavish copy of the old. For a start, the smaller wheels and deeper wings of the postwar cars made a difference to the proportions, and the two men also decided on a new rear-end treatment without the enclosed spare wheel. A metal cover over the hood well

A 1948 12 hp Tourer, with hood and sidescreens erected. Compare this with the earlier picture of the Tourer on page 10.

was also a refinement not seen on the Rover Tourers of the 1930s.

Though quite a pretty car, the Tourer was something of a compromise. The rather upright wings and bonnet of the postwar model and its standard disc wheels seemed to take away much of the sporting character of the original design, which the twin horns and central pass lamp of the Sports Saloon models did little to improve. The contours at the rear of the body were modified, probably after only a few cars had been built, and later Tourers had a more rounded tail. Body construction – still using metal panels on an ash frame – was always carried out by A.P. Aircraft Ltd, who rented a portion of Rover's Clay Lane factory for the purpose, but not many Tourers were made before production ceased at the end of 1947.

Even though these Rovers were selling to the buyer's market of the immediate postwar world, they never attained the sales volumes of their prewar counterparts. Partly, this must have been because they were elderly designs, and partly it was because Rover were obliged to export 50% of

all cars they built in 1946 and 75% in 1947 to meet Government legislation. As the cars had relatively little appeal in export markets, numbers remained low – and the Rover factories were reduced to working only four days a week in alternate weeks by May 1947.

Just 5,115 cars were built in 1946 and a further 8,220 in 1947, figures which compared with nearly 11,000 cars built in 1939. It was not enough to fill the large Solihull factory and not enough to ensure Rover's survival, and it was the reason why Maurice Wilks quickly drew up a little four-wheel-drive utility vehicle which he hoped would sell well overseas and tide Rover over until better trading conditions returned. The Land-Rover, introduced in 1948, rapidly went on to outsell the Rover saloons by two to one and become the Rover Company's principal product. Before that occurred, however, Rover would introduce the new range of saloons which had provided much of the running-gear for the Land-Rover. These were the P3s, announced as Rover's 1948 models and the direct replacements for the revived prewar cars.

# CHAPTER 2

# Inlets over exhausts

## The P3 gap-filler, 1948 – 1949

**P3 60 and 75 (1948-49)**

Once the war was over and the Rover Company could legitimately think again in terms of new models, they were confronted by an awkward problem which faced all European manufacturers. American car design had not been interrupted by the hostilities until 1942, and was now three years ahead. The 1946-season American cars were radically different in appearance from the immediate prewar European models, and although they were few and far between on this side of the Atlantic, it was clear that all the advances of those three lost years had to be assimilated in record time if the new European models were not to look, and be, horribly dated in comparison.

Maurice Wilks' first serious plan was for a much modified P2, re-engined with a new IOE unit derived from Jack Swaine's V6 of the mid-1930s. This engine had been running in prototype four-cylinder form before the war, and could soon be brought up to production standard, although it was broader than the '100mm' OHV units, and so the P2 chassis frame would have to be widened at the front. As for the body, it would simply be the standard P2 style, widened and updated with a new front end based on the American styling trends of 1942. This meant a full-width front with wings blending into the radiator grille panel. Aided as usual by Harry Loker, Wilks tried out various styling modifications in clay on a full-size P2, but somehow a full-width front in the 1942 American idiom always looked comical grafted on to a prewar Rover passenger cabin. As Rover could not wait too long before putting a new model into the showrooms, Wilks abandoned the project and decided to try something else.

There was no doubt in his mind that the new car should have an IOE engine with the existing production gearbox (which had recently been redesigned for the P2 models), but instead of rejigging the old underslung chassis frame Rover could use the new, more rigid frame which had been under development in 1939 and had run throughout the war in prototype form with the body of a 10hp. To this could be added independent front suspension, for Rover had done a lot of work on such systems since the mid-1930s. As there was no time to start work on a completely new body, the widened P2 body would have to do, with a nose design generally similar to the prewar one. This second attempt at a postwar Rover became the production P3.

As things were to turn out, designing the P3 was rather more complicated than it appeared at first sight, especially when Wilks decided to go for an all-steel body instead of the ash-framed type of P2s. Yet despite the major engineering changes which went into the P3, it was obvious to Rover from the outset that a car which looked so much like the prewar models could only be a stop-gap, even in the seller's market presented by a car-starved world in the early postwar years. Indeed, P3 production was to last no longer than 18 months.

## Chassis and engines

'In order to gear production to the National need for economy,' read the P3 sales catalogue, 'the Rover Company decided to produce one chassis model only with a choice of four- or six-cylinder engines.' That single chassis had a wheelbase of 110½in, midway between the wheelbase lengths of the P2 10 and 12 and considerably shorter than that of the superseded 14 and 16. Its track was an inch wider at the rear than that of the P2, while the front track was half-an-inch narrower. Although of massively rigid box-section construction, which obviated the need for the harmonic stabilizer, it was actually lighter than the P2 chassis because it reached only three-quarters of the way under the car; the side members stopped short at the rear spring hanger mounting, and the springs themselves were then mounted at their rear ends to a crossmember attached to the rear of the body. This curious arrangement had originally been thought out by Gordon Bashford as a way of getting round the limited rear wheel rebound movement of the underslung P2 chassis; if an upswept frame led to space

A ⅟₁₆th scale model, dated July 1945, of a 'Proposed new saloon'. Despite the remarkably well-balanced styling, the proposal was never taken seriously, and seems not to have progressed to a full-size mock-up. Possibly Rover feared the cost of developing and tooling-up for such a radically new shape – or possibly they thought the British public was not ready for it!

The earliest full-size mock-ups of what was simply called a 'Proposed new car' date from November 1945. This spectacularly grotesque front end was built up on a prewar bodyshell which had simply been sawn down the middle and widened – the clay which disguised the join can just be seen.

By December 1945 the front end design had been tamed a little, although the horrible American-style bumpers are still in evidence. A contemporary note in the Rover archives describes this as 'P3'; later mock-ups are described as 'model P' or, again, 'Proposed new car'.

Some sanity appeared to be returning by January 1946...

reduction in the body, and an underslung frame gave suspension problems, then the obvious answer had to be no frame at all! Original ideas like this tended to go unnoticed in an era when the motoring public was less technically minded than it is now, but they do go to show just how much innovative thinking was being applied beneath the conventional exterior of Rover's cars.

Although the Girling independent front suspension was new to Rovers, it was basically similar to that which Lanchester had used on their Roadrider model in the 1930s. Rover had developed it to suit their own needs, first for the M-type economy car of 1945-46, which never got beyond the prototype stage, and now for the P3. It used lever-type hydraulic shock absorbers to form the top wishbone, set at an angle to lend the geometry a degree of anti-dive action, together with long radius arms at the bottom. It soon became apparent that the system gave poor control of small wheel movements, however, and engineer George Mackie remembers removing front wings from test

...and this version was proposed in February. Only the grille, bumper and bumper valance details differ from the production P3.

Also proposed in February 1946 was this full-width front design.

cars so that he could watch what was happening while someone else drove! For the 1949 season, a two-piece wishbone replaced the piston-type dampers, and telescopic shock absorbers were fitted. At the same time, the radius arms were lengthened, and they now pivoted from the chassis crossmember which also supported the gearbox. Throughout P3 production, rubber bushes between suspension linkages and chassis were used to minimize noise transmission, and in conjunction with pre-packed bearings they helped reduce the need for lubrication to such an extent that the automatic chassis lubrication system of the P2s was no longer necessary.

The independent front suspension meant that it was no longer practicable to use rod-operated brakes, but Maurice Wilks had such faith in the Girling system that he retained as much of it as he could; thus the P3s had hydraulic front brakes linked to the familiar rod-operated brakes at the rear.

This sort of compromise was typical of the era. Riley, for example, did the same for their first car with independent front suspension – the RM series of 1946 – and Rolls-Royce used a system very similar to the Rover one, but modified to accept servo actuation. Hydro-mechanical brakes were not universally successful, the Riley version being prone to all kinds of troubles, while even the Rover brakes were markedly less efficient at low speeds than the all-mechanical system of the P2s. Rover proudly quoted a stopping distance of 30ft from 30mph with properly set-up mechanical brakes; the P3 took 38ft to stop from the same speed. Wheels of 17in diameter were standard, but 16in wheels could be specified, and the P3 had a new recirculating ball steering system by Burman incorporating a variable ratio for the first time on a Rover, which had the welcome benefit of reducing effort at parking speeds.

The P3's engine deserves consideration in some detail,

Although this photograph is undated, it is generally thought to show another early postwar styling mock-up, despite the late 1930s wire wheels. Separate bonnet and wings are retained, but the nose has an unfamiliar shape, while the wings, running-boards and bumpers are new, and the boot lid treatment recalls the 1938-40 10hp Coupe.

The new engine had overhead inlet and side exhaust valves with a sloping cylinder head. The P3 units breathed through a Solex carburettor.

The IOE layout of the P3 engine is clearly shown in this picture of a Rover display unit. The separate inlet manifold and head castings would be changed for the P4.

because in one form or another it was to power Rover cars and Land-Rovers for over 30 years. The origins of the IOE design in the experimental V6 engine of the mid-1930s have already been discussed. The first in-line example was running before the war, and as soon as peacetime development work could begin again it was to the IOE layout that Maurice Wilks turned. A scaled-down four-cylinder IOE engine of 699cc was built to power the M-type prototypes in 1945, but the first production applications were in 60bhp, 1,595cc four-cylinder form and in 72bhp, 2,103cc six-cylinder form in the P3 60 and P3 75 models. Just a few weeks after their introduction, a detuned version of the four-cylinder engine also went into production for the very first Land-Rovers.

From a design point of view, the sloping-head inlet-over-exhaust layout was ideal for the time. The extremely efficient combustion chamber shape meant that there were no problems over using the low-grade Pool petrol which was then all that was available in Britain. In comparison with the '100mm' engine, the IOE unit was more flexible, its consumption of fuel was lower and it permitted quicker acceleration. It also promised quiet running for higher mileages, as a hydraulic timing chain tensioner prevented the familiar clatter of the high-mileage '100mm' engine from setting in; it was just as smooth, if not smoother, and it was extremely robust.

This interesting shot shows the P3's new front bumper and the pedestal-mounted pass lamp. GAC 915 was a pre-production vehicle and was first registered on October 2, 1947; it bears the grille badge of a 14hp model.

RAC ratings for the new four-cylinder and six-cylinder engines would have been 11.98hp and 15.81hp, respectively (and the long stroke of the design was a reminder that it had been conceived under the RAC system of taxation), but the new cars were given model designations based on the engines' actual power output, doubtless because the RAC system ceased to apply to cars built after 1946. Thus what in P2 terms would have been a four-cylinder 12 became a 60, and what would have been a six-cylinder 16 became a 75. Both had a dual-downdraught Solex carburettor like those fitted to the six-cylinder P2s. Six 75s were made with a triple-SU installation, which endowed the cars with much improved acceleration and a higher top speed than the standard model. The exact history of this variant remains obscure, although it has been said that the engines were experimental try-outs for the P4 75. Not that the standard cars were exactly sluggards; the 75 boasted a top speed of around 75mph, and the 60 could attain 72mph. In both cases, these speeds were reached more rapidly than by the equivalent 12s and 16s of 1947. It has already been seen that the two models used the same chassis; the shorter four-cylinder engine was simply set further back in the frame, giving the 60 rather less understeer than its six-cylinder cousin.

A look at production figures shows a drop of just over 2,000 cars for the first season of P3 production as compared with the final P2 season, and the 1949 season's total of 2,989 cars seems very low until one remembers that it

A four-light P3; by now, Rover had dropped the term Sports Saloon, although this particular example would certainly have been worthy of the name as its six-cylinder engine is fitted with triple carburettors.

represents the output for just over half a year, from January to August 1949. In fact, Solihull was working flat-out and total vehicle production had risen; the first Land-Rover was delivered in July 1948, and over 8,000 were built before the demise of the P3 in the autumn of 1949. Nevertheless, the P3 production total of 9,111 makes it the rarest of the classic Rovers.

## Bodies

The P3 body panels were stamped out by Pressed Steel, but the bodies were assembled by Rover at Solihull. The range of styles was limited to two – although a handful of dropheads were also built – and it is interesting to note that the designation Sports Saloon had disappeared from the Company's literature. In its place was a four-light Saloon, as an alternative to the six-light Saloon, and a new pricing policy meant that both bodies cost exactly the same on their respective chassis.

Although these bodies closely resembled the P2 Saloon and Sports Saloon, they actually shared very few common panels. The easiest way of seeing the difference is by comparing dimensions, when it becomes apparent that the P3 body was wider at the front and narrower at the back than its P2 counterpart. It also had less headroom and a slightly bigger boot. Overall, the 60 and 75 were shorter and wider than their predecessors, but the shorter wheelbase did not affect interior space as the P2 and P3 bodies were the same length. Twin horns and a pass lamp mounted on a central pillar ahead of the radiator helped to distinguish the new cars from their forebears at a quick glance.

Otherwise, there was little about P3 bodies worthy of comment. The facia arrangement and controls echoed P2 practice, the tool kit was still in a tray under the dashboard, and a sliding roof and louvres over the drop-glasses continued to be provided. Improved ventilation with heater/demister ducting built into the bodyshell did away

The P3 was readily recognizable from behind by its chrome overriders and wing-mounted tail lights. The extra width of the all-steel body was also easily seen in the larger rear window.

with the need for an opening windscreen, and a small Rover emblem filled the space in the dashboard where the opening handle had been on P2s. Now that the windscreen did not open there was no need for the off-screen wiper parking facility, and the independent control of the two wipers disappeared. The main lighting switch moved from the dashboard to the left-hand side of the steering column and,

following the practice of the final P2s, there was provision for the fitting of a radio in the dash; in some cases cars were factory-fitted with the Radiomobile Model 100 set. Probably the most noticeable interior difference from the P2s, however, was the use of plain leather seat facings in place of the more expensive ribbed type; not surprisingly, P3 seats were not as comfortable as their forebears.

The 1948 75 Graber Tourer, photographed when new. This car still survives in the hands of an enthusiast in the UK.

In 1948, Rover arranged for a six-light 75 Saloon to be fitted by Tickford with a drophead coupe body similar to that concern's efforts on 1939-40 models. Although the car was shown on the Rover stand at the 1948 Motor Show, and two further examples were built later that year on specially-earmarked chassis, nothing further came of these experiments, the P4's arrival in autumn 1949 putting paid to any plans there may have been for production drophead bodies on the P3 chassis.

Not surprisingly, the odd three-quarter chassis of the P3 did not attract the specialist coachbuilders and, indeed, Rover did not offer the car in chassis-only form.

Nevertheless, in September 1948, Baumberger and Voster, the Swiss Rover agents, managed to obtain a right-hand-drive export chassis (number R8431157) on behalf of Herr Voster, who passed it to the coachbuilder Graber, in Zurich, and asked for a unique Tourer body to be built on it. A slab-sided body of semi-streamlined appearance (ultra-modern by contemporary standards) was duly built, and the car was shown on Graber's stand at the 1949 Geneva Motor Show. After a succession of owners, it came to Britain in 1962 and still exists, although it is not on the road at the time of writing. No other special-bodied P3s are known to have been built.

# CHAPTER 3

# The 'Auntie' Rover

## Cyclops and successors, 1949 – 1964

**P4 60** (1953-1959), **75** (1949-1959), **80** (1959-1962), **90** (1953-1959), **95** (1962-1964), **100** (1959-1962), **105** (1958-1959), **105R and 105S** (1956-1958), **110** (1962-1964)

The all-new postwar Rover finally materialized in 1949. Too late to affect the final shape of the P3, a new American car had been launched which in Maurice Wilks' view embodied the sort of proportions he could see as a Rover. As usual, he wanted a pattern to work from, and this time he found it in the 1947 Studebakers.

These Studebakers, in fact, had far-reaching effects on body design in the motor industry as a whole. Styled by the industrial designer Raymond Loewy in conjunction with Studebaker's Virgil Exner, they represented a new departure, in which bonnet, wings and body were no longer considered as separate entities; instead, there was a full-width bodyshell with slab sides from front to rear, and visual relief provided only by contour lines pressed into the panels. At the rear, the boot echoed and balanced the bonnet, to give what someone christened the 'going-both-ways' look. Maurice Wilks got his hands on one as soon as he could, and a 1948-model Studebaker Champion duly arrived at Solihull. Its body was stripped from its chassis and was fitted to the first P4 development chassis which, by a happy coincidence, shared the Studebaker's dimensions almost exactly. The so-called 'Roverbaker' ran as a development vehicle for many years and was eventually rebuilt as a Studebaker again and used as a works hack.

Maurice Wilks set to work with Harry Loker to design the new Rover's body on the basis of the Studebaker. For the first time they used clay models instead of modifying full-size cars. The new body took shape, aping the 'going-both-ways' look and the four-light design of the Studebaker, but settling for rather less boxy styling and a pleasantly tapering boot line. The nose styling caused some headaches, as the garish grille of the Studebaker was clearly unsuitable and a traditional Rover grille was out of the question. One series of clay models had low-mounted headlamps behind perspex covers, but eventually the final full-size mock-up settled for a rather stark arrangement with the radiator grille's horizontal slats painted in the body colour and a Cyclopean pass lamp (carried over from the P3's separately-mounted lamp) recessed into the centre of the grille; head and side lamps were to be mounted in the wings. Thus the new car appeared in the autumn of 1949, its new and curious frontal aspect causing many a broken heart among devotees of the 'classic' Rover style exemplified by the P3s and the models of the later 1930s. The P4, however, was quite up-to-the-minute in styling; the delay had enabled Rover to base it on the 1947-season American fashion, while rivals like Standard, who had been quicker off the mark after the war, were stuck with models based on the outmoded 1942 style.

### Chassis and engines

The P4's chassis was developed directly from that used in the P3 and was available in both left-hand and right-hand-drive form like its predecessor. Reasoning no doubt that the

Three different quarter-scale models were made for the P4, and were known as 500, 501 and 502, after the registration numbers painted on them. This is 500, which had an interesting chrome rubbing strip along the sides to match the bumpers. Headlamps are enclosed behind perspex covers, the grille design is odd, and a split windscreen is in evidence, but the general lines of the P4 are already there.

P4 production lines, *circa* 1950. The cars in this picture are later Cyclops model 75s, with the eight-bar grille.

The IOE engine and gearbox of a P4, pictured in 1953. This particular one was probably a development unit, as production examples did not have the curious plate visible here on the inlet manifold. The general appearance of the IOE engine remained unchanged throughout the P4's life, although there were variations in carburation, air cleaning arrangements, fan blades and, of course, the number of cylinders.

quality of postwar steel boded ill for the future of the P3s, with their rear springs mounted directly to the body, Gordon Bashford this time specified a full-length frame with the massive side-members gracefully upswept over the rear axle. The familiar semi-elliptic springs took care of the rear suspension, while the P3's IFS in its final form was retained at the front. Steering was once again Burman recirculating ball-type, although the six-cylinder P4s were always characterized by heavy understeer, the result of moving the engine forward in the frame to get more interior length than in the P3 within the same wheelbase.

In these essentials, the P4 chassis remained unchanged for the full 15 years of its production, and the major model differences were almost entirely related to the engines, which (very roughly) lent their power output figures as model designations. At first only one model was available, the 75, with 2,103cc six-cylinder engine. This differed from the P3 engine of the same capacity by its one-piece lightweight aluminium cylinder head and manifold, chromium-plated cylinder bores, and external oil filtration system through a Wipac filter mounted high up on the cylinder head. Twin SU carburettors with an oil-bath air cleaner replaced the dual-choke Solex of the P3, giving a slight increase in power, plus greater flexibility through increased torque.

The 75 was joined in autumn 1953 by the four-cylinder 60, one rung below it in the Rover hierarchy, and by the 90, a larger-engined 'six' one rung above. The requirement for 90bhp in this latter model, which was originally intended primarily for export, had led indirectly to a number of changes in the basic IOE engine design, because although the unit had been designed as a 'stretchable' one, the amount of over-boring necessary to extract the extra 15bhp

Rover liked to exhibit cutaway engines, and this photo shows a display version of the odd man out among P4 engines – the OHV 80 unit. The long transmission casing incorporates an overdrive.

led to siamesed bores. Rover built an experimental batch of 30 75s in 1950 with engines over-bored to 2,638cc, but the favoured customers to whom they went reported piston ring scuffing if the cars were driven really hard. So Joe Drinkwater, head of the Drawing Office's engine section, suggested that the cylinder bore centres could be repositioned within the block to leave more metal between each bore and thus give better cooling.

This 'spread bore' arrangement met with approval despite the additional complication of reducing the width of both big-end and main bearings as compared to the 75 engine. The production 'spread bore' engine consequently had bearings of tougher material than the 75's to cope with the increased unit loading. In six-cylinder 90 form, it developed 90bhp from 2,638cc, with an even lower compression ratio

than the 75's, which hinted that Rover might have a higher-performance version in mind for later. The 60 had 60bhp from a 1,997cc 'spread bore' engine with the same low compression ratio. Both engines used a single carburettor, the 60 breathing through a conventional oil-wetted gauze air cleaner, while the 90 (and export 60s) had a Vokes paper-element air cleaner; both had a rather more efficient oil filtration system than the 2,103cc engine. The 90's compression ratio was raised slightly in 1954, and then again in 1955 to give a 93bhp output, which the model would retain until its demise in 1959.

It obviously made sense to redesign the 75's engine along the same lines, and in the autumn of 1955 the 75 duly received its 'spread-bore' engine. Of slightly larger capacity than the earlier unit, this 2,230cc engine developed 80bhp (it

28

This picture, taken in August 1949, shows the first production P4 chassis. Note the massive side members and the rigid bracing of the frame. The P4 was the last production Rover car to have a separate chassis. In the background, the old guard is represented by a splendid Sports Saloon of the mid-1930s and a four-light P3.

The original P4 75 was a particularly handsome car. This photograph shows the central pass lamp, which earned it the nickname Cyclops.

is not clear why the model was not redesignated an 80) and gave much improved torque characteristics with a consequent increase in flexibility. Its single carburettor, breathing now through a Vokes paper-element air cleaner (although Export models, like 1956 Export 90s, had an oil-bath type), must have let Maurice Wilks and Jack Swaine sleep more easily, as experience with the original 75 had taught them that all the advantage of multiple-carburettor systems was lost if they were not regularly and competently tuned. That admitted, the next P4 engine was nevertheless to have twin carburettors!

The fourth and fifth P4 models arrived in autumn 1956, both using a twin-carburettor, high-compression version of the 90's engine which gave 108bhp. Oil-bath air cleaners had returned in January 1956 to Home Market 75s and 90s, and were fitted to the two 105 variants which, by virtue of their performance and fittings, immediately took over from the 90 at the top of the P4 range. If the 105S was quicker than the 90, however, it was also thirstier. Both the 105R and the 105S sold tolerably well for such expensive vehicles, but

The early P4s had a small rear window and a sloping boot lid. The circular reflectors on this 1950 Cyclops were added later, when red reflectors at the rear became a legal requirement. Photograph by Alan Milstead.

The Cyclops front end was discarded in 1952. This 1956 season 90 displays the replacement design, with the addition of the torpedo-style side lamps which had arrived in September 1954. 1952 and some 1953 models had chromed grille slats instead of the anodized aluminium type later standardized.

A larger boot, new tail lights and a three-piece wrap-around window arrived on 1955 season cars.

there is no doubt that the petrol rationing which followed the Suez crisis of 1957 did irreparable damage to their sales potential. The 105R was particularly badly affected, probably because its automatic transmission made it wasteful of fuel, and Rover dropped it from the range with something approaching relief when, in autumn 1958, the new P5 3-litre was able to offer an automatic option. The 105S became a 105 for 1959 and then disappeared altogether, along with its 60, 75 and 90 stablemates.

Inevitably, the arrival of the 3-litre had its effect on the existing saloon car range. One projected P4 model in the late 1950s had the 3-litre engine with Borg-Warner automatic transmission and power-assisted steering, but this disappeared from view when persistent trouble with camshafts and rockers in the existing P4 engines encouraged the Engineering Department to concentrate instead on developing a new 2.6-litre engine from the 3-litre unit, which used a redesigned and more robust valve train. Once the P5 3-litre was available, the P4 assumed a new position as the 'cheaper' Rover, and there was obviously no point in having three six-cylinder cars as close in specification as the 75, 90 and 105 as second-string models. So for the 1960 season, the six-cylinder models were cut back to one, and the new 100 featured the 2,625cc engine which had been developed from the 3-litre unit. The latter was itself a development of the 'spread-bore' 90 engine with cylinder centres again repositioned, a seven-bearing crankshaft, and roller cam followers in place of the original pad type. Fitted with a single SU carburettor, the 100 engine was essentially a short-stroke 3-litre unit, with a power output of 104bhp. Once again, flexibility and torque had been improved, although – test results by the motoring journals notwithstanding – the 100 was not quite as quick as the superseded 105, even if it was marginally more frugal in its consumption of petrol.

31

Also introduced in the autumn of 1959 was the 80, a four-cylinder replacement for the 60. It was the only P4 not to use a variant of the IOE engine, having instead a 2,286cc OHV engine similar to that in the contemporary Land-Rover and developed from the Land-Rover's 2,052cc diesel unit. In cubic capacity, this engine was actually larger than that of the six-cylinder 75, so to some extent the 80 may also be said to have replaced the cheapest of the superseded six-cylinder range. Developing 77bhp and fitted with a Solex carburettor breathing through the by now customary oil-bath air cleaner, the OHV unit made the 80 slightly quicker than the 60 it replaced, but the Land-Rover engine did betray some of its agricultural origins and there was a problem with timing-chain noise in the earlier examples. Nevertheless, the four-cylinder engine was mounted further back in the chassis than the 'sixes', with the result that the 80 suffered less from the characteristic P4 understeer.

The 80 and 100 were christened 'Mk IV' models when the new chassis numbering system arrived in June 1961 (although no-one seems to know why). Both survived until autumn 1962, when they were replaced by two new six-cylinder models based on the 100, which were destined to be the last P4s of all. With impeccable logic, these were known as 'Mk I' models! The 95's engine was identical to that of the 100 except for a valve timing revision which put power down to 102bhp and enabled use of a higher axle ratio, while the new 110 was fitted with the redesigned cylinder head and inlet manifold which had been developed for the 3-litre, and with that car's larger carburettor and paper-element air cleaner. Since 1949, the IOE engines had had a lightweight one-piece head and manifold casting, which was relatively cheap to produce but permitted little tuning. By using separate castings for head and manifold, Rover found they were able to cast more efficient shapes for the inlet manifold tracts. The inlet port shape was reworked by performance development expert Harry Weslake, and the resulting so-called 'Weslake head' gave the 110's engine a maximum power output of 123bhp, the highest of all the P4s. The 110's acceleration was consequently quite as good as that of the twin-carburettor 105 and 105S, and its claimed

This 100 shows the later style of two-tone paint, and the new hubcaps with dished centres which came in with the disc-braked cars. The recessed front grille and new bumpers had been introduced in 1958 to give the P4 closer visual links with the P5 3-litre.

top speed of nearly 106mph made it the fastest P4 of all in that respect. Sadly, it was also the thirstiest.

The very first 75s had a hydro-mechanical braking system similar to that of the P3, but with twin leading shoes instead of leading-and-trailing shoes at the front. From autumn 1950 a fully hydraulic all-drum system was standard, which from the 1956 season was improved by the use of shorter linings designed to prevent grabbing or knocking while reversing. The 1956-59 90s, and all 105 variants, had twin trailing shoes at the front. Servo assistance arrived for the 1956 season, but was initially confined to overdrive-equipped 90s because Solihull reasoned that if the engine stalled on a freewheeling servo-equipped car, a panic-stricken driver might exhaust the servo and find himself with neither brakes nor engine braking. The servo was standard on the 105R and 105S models, and remained so until the demise of the 105 in 1959. After autumn 1959, all models had servo-assisted brakes as standard, with Girling discs on the front wheels in place of the original drums. Disc-braked cars had dished wheel rims so that the wheels should not protrude

beyond the bodywork; in order to maintain the same track, this meant that the rear axle had to be widened slightly. The disc-braked cars could be specified with wider 6.40-section tyres instead of the 6.00-section tyres which remained standard until the end of P4 production. These fatter tyres, still on the 15in wheels which the P4 had always used, tended to make the steering heavier at parking speeds, and a lower steering box ratio was standardized in autumn 1960 to redress the balance.

One of the P4's more endearing idiosyncrasies was its handbrake. Sited outboard and ahead of the driver so that a bench front seat could be fitted, it was initially the subject of complaint from customers who found that they could not reach it. Rover added a rearward extension during the 1950 season, giving the lever its famous 'shepherd's crook' configuration, and then had second thoughts for 1954, specifying a pull-up lever positioned between the driver's seat and the door. This seems to have met with considerable market resistance, with the result that the 'shepherd's crook' was reinstated for 1955 and, after a further small

A 1959 75, showing the extra chrome added over the rear number-plate for that season.

much to be desired in comparison with the gear change of P3 and earlier Rovers, and its sobriquet of 'pot-stirrer' is adequately descriptive! The long, cranked handle was so designed in order to leave legroom for a third passenger on the bench front seat; certainly not made for fast changing, it was nevertheless adjustable to suit the driver's reach, and Rover never changed it until the end, even employing the same design on the first P5 3-litre cars.

The P4 gearbox was essentially that of the P3, with a raised third gear ratio to give better acceleration. Synchromesh covered third and fourth gears only until autumn 1953, when it was added to second as well, but it was never extended to first. Prior to the arrival of the 80 and 100 models in autumn 1959, gearboxes featured the Rover freewheel, except that Laycock DeNormanville overdrive was optionally available instead on the 90 from autumn 1955, on the 60 and 75 from the following year, and was standard on the 105S/105 models. Both 80 and 100 models

modification for 1956, remained unchanged until the end of production.

Gear levers were also below previous Rover standards on the P4. Instead of the tidy floor-mounted lever of the P3s, the first P4s had an American-style column change, which was woolly in the extreme. It was far from universally appreciated, and a floor-change conversion was offered by Gethin's, the Rover distributors in Birmingham. This conversion, which was found particularly on Police models but was otherwise rare, seems to have been brought to Gethin's by Peter Wilks, one of the progenitors of the P4 75-based Marauder sports car, which had an almost identical gear change.

The purpose of the column change was of course also to make room for the bench front seat, but Rover finally gave in to customer pressure and fitted a new floor-mounted gear lever for the 1954 season, coinciding with the introduction of the 60 and 90 models. It has to be said that this still left

This magnificent 1964 110 was overall prizewinner at the 1982 Rover P4 Drivers' Guild's National Concours. The 110 was the only P4 to have the later 3-litre type wheel covers.

An unusual shot, taken in June 1949, of a P4 prototype without its doors. The plain leather seat facings and generous leg room all round are well illustrated. Note the angular overriders, which differed from the production items, the 15-bar grille and the extra chrome around headlights and air intakes.

had overdrive as standard (although it was only standardized at the very last moment, and a small number of early cars were built without it, having a four-speed gearbox with no freewheel) and all 110 models had overdrive. For those who wanted better acceleration and more relaxed cruising, a high 3.9:1 axle ratio was introduced in 1955 as an option for the non-overdrive 90, and was actually more common than is generally supposed. The 3.9 axle returned on the 95, the only manual-transmission model offered with neither overdrive nor freewheel.

Various semi-automatic and preselector gearboxes had been available in Britain since the 1930s, and indeed Rover's own freewheel could be seen as a form of semi-automatic in that it offered clutchless gear changing. By the mid-1950s, however, fully automatic transmissions were just beginning to catch on in the upper regions of the UK market; Rolls-Royce, for example, had introduced theirs in 1954. Rover decided to follow this American-inspired trend, linking an automatic gearbox to the torquiest of the P4 engines in the 105R. They preferred to design and build

their own automatic gearbox rather than use an expensive imported unit, and the Roverdrive transmission fitted to the 105R is a fascinating representative of Britain's home-grown answers to the American automatic gearboxes. Unfortunately, Rover were not able to install it without incurring a cost penalty; their transmission was so long that the 105R had to have special chassis alterations to accommodate it!

Like modern automatic transmissions, the Roverdrive had a torque convertor behind the flywheel, but this used oil from the sump. Behind it was a servo-operated single-dry-plate clutch, a two-speed-and-reverse manual gearbox, and then an overdrive set to cut in automatically. Normally, the car would start in 'Intermediate' (the top gear of the main box) and the overdrive would take over at higher speeds; a manual override gave selection of 'Emergency Low', or the bottom gear of the synchromesh box, to give more torque for climbing steep hills or more engine braking for descending them. The Roverdrive unit was long-lived and generally reliable; its main problem was that it endowed the 108bhp 105R with acceleration little better than the

An interior view of an early Cyclops. The rectangular instruments disappeared after a single season, and an extension was added to the handbrake lever even before that, but the column gear change would remain until 1953.

considerably cheaper 60bhp 60 model. It was not universally liked at Solihull, either; Jack Swaine scornfully dismisses its acceleration as 'pathetic'. Nevertheless, as the first ever automatic Rover, it holds a special place in the Company's history.

**Bodies**

The basic shape of the P4 body, and in particular its passenger cabin, did not alter between 1949 and 1964, so that a 'Cyclops' is instantly recognizable as the elder sister of a 95 or 110. All the shells were built by Pressed Steel at Cowley, originally with door, bonnet and boot lid panels of Birmabright aluminium alloy. As introduced in the autumn of 1949, the P4 75 had the 'Cyclops' nose, featuring a 15-bar radiator grille and chrome trimming around the headlamps and air intake grilles. This chrome trimming rapidly disappeared, and the 15-bar grille went out in favour of a similar one with only eight bars after overheating problems showed up. From behind, these early cars were distinguished by a small oval window similar to that of the P3,

horizontal tail lamps, and a sloping boot lid with a square number-plate box and a large vertical handle. A look inside revealed a bench seat at the front and a full-width dashboard with rectangular instruments ahead of the driver. The stalk switches on the steering column for lights and indicators were new to Rovers, and the bench front seat had brought with it that American-style column gear change and the handbrake lever displaced to somewhere by the driver's right knee (or left knee on LHD cars). The semi-circular horn ring on the steering wheel was American in origin, too. Both outside and inside the car there were new pushbutton door handles, those inside doubling as door pulls, but the polished walnut dashboard and door cappings, the deep pile carpets, and of course the leather seats, were all in the familiar Rover mould, although the plain seat facings of the P3 had been retained.

By the standards of the day, the 75 was a very well-equipped car, but Rover offered a number of optional extras. Owners could specify additional wheel trim rings ('rimbellishers'), a badge bar mounted between the over-

Pleated leather first appeared for the 1956 season. A bench front seat is fitted to this car, although individual seats had also become available. The circular instrument faces had arrived in 1950 and the 'pot-stirrer' gear lever in 1953.

riders, and a windscreen washer kit. Louder windtone horns were available and the passenger compartment could be furnished with footrests for the rear, floor mats, a cigarette lighter and either felt or plastic seat covers.

Even so, Solihull did not get the new style right first time. As already noted, the handbrake lever had to be modified during the 1950 season, and the rectangular instruments were also not well-received, so that circular dials replaced them from autumn 1950. At the same time, the clock moved to the centre of the wooden facia rail. In addition, the doors gained rising hinges, orthodox interior handles in place of the pushbutton type, and their courtesy lights were rewired to operate independently of the side lamps.

A number of radical revisions were introduced in March 1952. Most immediately apparent was a new front end, with a chromed grille bearing a triangular badge similar to that of

the P3s. The 'Cyclops' pass lamp had disappeared, and instead there were Lucas double-dipping headlamps to suit the new lighting regulations. The wing area around these lamps had been tidied up, and there was also a new valance between bumper and body. This new front end, which had really been necessitated by customer resistance to the original pattern, had also permitted a change in the heating and ventilating arrangements. The air intake was now mounted high up on the scuttle, where it would no longer pick up fumes and dust from the road, and was covered by a flap controlled from the dashboard. At the same time, the opportunity had been taken to fit a more powerful heater.

Small changes had also occurred at the rear; the rear window was wider and the number-plate box was rectangular, the overall result being that the car looked wider and lower from behind. The spare wheel was now accessible through a flap beneath the bumper, and the rear body mountings had been changed relative to the chassis so that there was an extra inch of headroom for back seat passengers. The seats themselves had improved springing, and a recess in the front seat back increased legroom for those behind. The driver's job was made easier by a more controllable organ-type accelerator pedal and self-parking windscreen wipers, while there was a new circular horn ring, and the low-fuel warning light was replaced by a reserve tap. In addition, there were changes to the lighting and freewheel controls.

Two-tone paint schemes put in their first appearance during 1953, but were limited to two; there was dark grey over light grey or dark green over light green, the upper colour covering the roof panel only. With the introduction of the 60 and 90 models for 1954 came a handbrake repositioned between the driver's seat and the door. The handy door pockets were deleted so that the driver's should not foul the new handbrake, and chromed interior door pull handles arrived a few months later in March 1954. The 90 models were distinguished by a fog lamp mounted on the left-hand side of the front bumper, and by 'Rover 90' in elegant script on the bonnet sides and boot lid. Grille badges, of course, bore the appropriate model designation – 60, 75, or 90.

In the meantime, Maurice Wilks had realized that Rover needed a professional body stylist. It was all very well starting from the basis of another car and adapting the design to suit a Rover, but it was a process which could not continue indefinitely. In late 1953, Wilks took on David Bache, who had served his apprenticeship with Austin at Longbridge, with the intention of grooming him as Rover's stylist. At this time, thoughts were beginning to turn to new models at Solihull, and Bache prepared some new designs for Wilks' approval. Although there were those at Rover who were highly impressed, Bache recalls that Maurice Wilks was horrified, and reminded him that while these designs were very good, Rovers were supposed to be discreet, not eye-catching! It was quite clear that a P4 was going to have to look like a P4 for some time to come, and indeed Bache was only ever allowed to make subtle revisions

to update the body styling in subsequent years.

For the 1955 season he was able to give the P4 bodies a raised boot line and consequent increase in luggage space, along with a much wider wrap-around rear window, divided into three sections, no doubt because Maurice Wilks had reservations about the strength of large areas of curved glass. Flashing trafficators were now beginning to replace semaphore arms, and recent legislation demanded red reflectors at the rear, so Bache killed two birds with one stone by combining trafficators, tail lights and reflectors in new vertical clusters at the rear. He gave the old front side lamps larger lenses and made them trafficators, while the side lamps emerged on top of the wings in chromed housings. Together with these changes came a widening of the two-tone paint options, better door sealing, and the provision of body touch-up pencils in the tool tray. The handbrake returned to its former position after attracting unfavourable comment in its 1954 location, and the door pockets were reinstated, although the economy-model 60 kept its pocketless door panels.

1956-season changes focussed on the interior, where pleated seat coverings and optional individual front seats were finally introduced, the former having been absent from Rovers since the arrival of the P3 in 1948. Apart from a change from clear to amber front indicator lenses, external revisions had to wait until the 1957 season, when a tidier front wing design by David Bache represented the first of a series of revisions intended to stress the family resemblance between the P4 and the as yet unreleased P5 3-litre. Meanwhile, the 90 lost its distinguishing fog lamp, and the new 105S and 105R De Luxe were fitted with twin fog lamps. These latter models both had rimbellishers and a cigar lighter as standard. Many 105R De Luxe models also had the optional rear footrests, which were otherwise rare, and this probably reflects the car's attraction as a chauffeur-driven vehicle.

All three 105 models had bonnet and boot lid badging in a rather less attractive script than the 90's, and there were, of course, distinguishing grille badges, that of the 105R being in yellow-and-brown instead of the red-and-black traditional to Rovers since 1930. The new models had plastic grille

The dashboard of a 105R, showing the unusual gear selector lever. Pressing the button in the knob activated the servo-operated clutch.

At the end, the P4 came to share the 3-litre's seat design. These non-reclining seats are on an 80, 95 or 100, but fully reclining seats of the same pattern were available on 110s and the later 95s.

badges, and the enamel badges of the older models were gradually phased out in favour of plastic ones, beginning in 1957 with the 90. Inside, the recessed door pockets fitted since 1954 to the 75 and 90 were replaced by flat pockets, which were also added to the 60 and found on the 105R and 105S models.

P4 changes for the 1958 season were limited in number, and to some extent were intended to pave the way for the 3-litre. The seats were given padded rolls at the edges, covered with plain leather, which greatly improved passenger location when cornering, and there was a revised gear selector quadrant for the 105R, with a rubber mat on the car's gearbox cover to resist the wear caused by the driver's idle left foot. The wool headlining was replaced in January 1958 by a washable plastic one available in only two colours. Outside, changes clearly envisaged earlier were introduced, and the two-tone colour scheme now divided along the top of the wings, giving a greater area for the upper colour. A chromed dividing strip was added, which became optional on the single-colour cars as well after December 1957. The 60 now received its plastic grille badge, leaving only the 75 with the earlier enamel variety.

The P5 3-litre was introduced in the autumn of 1958, and P4 models for 1959 were given the final stage of their facelift to underline the family resemblance. New bumpers and overriders, together with a recessed radiator grille and new-style 'Rover' nameplate, all followed the P5 pattern. A chromed embellisher above the rear number-plate again echoed the P5 design, and had the useful benefit of making the cars appear lower and wider from behind. All models now had the chrome side trim strip as standard, and an interior revision added a padded roll to the dashboard top, partly in a reflection of the 3-litre design, but also to some extent for safety reasons. The 105 could be distinguished from its 105S predecessor both by new badging and by the absence of that model's twin fog lamps and rimbellishers; inside, it had also lost the cigar lighter.

From the time of the appearance in autumn 1959 of the 80 and 100 models, P4 bodies changed very little indeed, and then only in badging and interior details. The 100 had script badging on its bonnet and boot lid, while the 80 had only its grille badge as identification. Both models had a key-operated starter switch in place of the pushbutton type, but otherwise changes from previous models were confined to small details such as the provision of interior coat hooks and the arrival in autumn 1961 of twin ashtrays instead of the single central type in the back of the front bench seats. These cars had 3-litre style recessed-centre hubcaps, and a new type of badge bar was introduced for them because the old type could not be fitted with the post-1958 overriders.

More major changes had to wait until 1962, when the 95 and 110 models shared with the revised P5 3-litres larger, clearer instrument dials with black instead of chrome bezels, spade-shaped switches, and instrument voltage stabilization. The 110 had rear arm slings and was available optionally with reclining individual front seats. Identification of both models was by chrome script badges in the usual places, although grille badges came from the 3-litre and consequently bore no model number. The 95 also had recessed-centre hubcaps, while the 110 had the larger wheel covers introduced on the 3-litre in 1961.

Crushable sun visors replaced the translucent plastic type during the 1963 season, and a picnic table made by an accessory manufacturer was offered as a new optional extra. It fitted over the gearbox cover, and remained rare. From March 1963, the Birmabright alloy body panels were replaced by heavier steel panels for reasons which have never been satisfactorily explained (perhaps it was more important to divert the supplies of alloy to the P6, which had both bonnet and boot lid of this material). Final detail changes came in the 1964 season, when both models received the cold-start switch of the 3-litre, and reclining seats became an option for the 95. Rover also approved a Webasto fabric sunroof for that season, and a number of 95s and 110s were so fitted.

**Experiments and prototypes**
Although the production P4s never wavered from the stolid four-light body which earned them their nickname of 'Auntie' – they represented the same staid respectability in the 1950s as did 'Auntie' BBC – Solihull was not short of alternative ideas. As early as 1950-51, a two-door drophead version was under consideration, and the two prototypes built by Salmons-Tickford, who of course had supplied the prewar drophead bodies, looked uncommonly like the gas turbine car JET 1. This car, described later, may well have been the source of inspiration. No-one at Rover seems to know why these elegant three-position dropheads never went into production. Next on the experimental list may have been a fixed-head coupe model, although it is possible that the contemporary witness who described this car as 'short' and 'round-backed' in fact confused it with a proposed Road Rover design on the P4 chassis.

The best-known of the proposed alternative body styles for the P4, however, is that designed in 1953 by Farina. The Turin concern was approached by the Rover Company some time late in 1952, and crafted a beautiful two-door drophead body for the P4 in the typical contemporary Italian idiom. This was fitted to a 75 chassis, and a fixed-head version was built shortly afterwards and fitted to a 90 chassis. The

Known at Solihull as the Rover Coupe, this is one of two prototype dropheads based on Cyclops 75s which were constructed in 1950-51 by Salmons-Tickford. They had two doors in place of the standard car's four, special pleated leather seat coverings and a split-squab arrangment at the front to permit rear access. At least one still survives, but in a very dilapidated condition.

The Farina drophead was attractively finished in metallic gold with a red convertible top. It still exists, albeit in rebuilt form, in the hands of an enthusiast.

Farina's fixed-head coupe on the P4 90 chassis served as the starting-point for P5 styling. The car was eventually sold to a Rover concessionaire in Spain, and is thought to have been written off in an accident.

drophead was shown on the Rover stand at the 1953 London Motor Show with the intention of gauging public reaction. Considerable interest was shown, and Rover commissioned a copy of the car (probably just the one, although a persistent rumour suggests two) from the Mulliner Coachbuilding Company in Birmingham. Sadly, this showed that production costs would be far too high, and the project was cancelled. Nevertheless, the Farina bodies were the underlying inspiration when Maurice Wilks tasked David Bache with designing the body for the P5 3-litre.

After that, Rover fought shy of special bodies, probably as much because space at Solihull was limited after the runaway success of the Land-Rover as because they feared the concomitant high costs. Nevertheless, the story is told of one other P4 drophead of the mid-1950s, supposedly built by Graber, in Switzerland, and evaluated at Solihull sometime around 1957. An eye-witness describes it as a dark green car which resembled Graber's design for the contemporary Alvis, but no further traces have yet been found. As for estate cars, Rover do not seem to have considered the P4 suitable for conversion (it was high and narrow, which would have handicapped it against contemporaries like the Humber estates), although at least one estate car was built in

1960 on a P4 100 chassis, allegedly by apprentices at Solihull. This car had a wooden-framed rear body, similar in construction to that of the Morris Minor Traveller.

Of course, the P4 was used extensively as a testbed for other components. In the early 1950s, the V6 engine proposed for the P5 was road-tested in a series of P4s, although none were made available to the public. At least one P4 was fitted in the later 1950s with a Land-Rover diesel engine (initially 2,052cc, later 2,286cc), and opposing views from the Experimental Department say it was either for mileage testing or in prospect of an order for diesel P4 taxis from Brazil, which was never fulfilled because Solihull could not refine the engines sufficiently to meet their own high standards! There were also two very special vehicles based on P4s which were run by Gordon Bashford's Advanced Engineering team in the mid-1950s. One was built up as a monocoque structure in order to test P5 construction methods and had an experimental double-wishbone front suspension, while the second and later one was built up as a

This wooden-bodied estate car on a P4 100 chassis, photographed by Jim Ritson, still survives.

base unit, P6-fashion.

Last, but by no means least, the P4 formed the basis of Rover's experiments with gas turbine propulsion for road vehicles in the early 1950s. Once the Company's experiments in the early postwar period had resulted in the design of a gas turbine engine which appeared suitable for automobile use, Gordon Bashford was given the job of building the car into which to fit it. Rather than start from scratch with a new and expensive design, he simply adapted a P4 'Cyclops'. The gas turbine engine, too bulky for the P4's engine compartment, was installed amidships behind the front seats. This automatically reduced the car to a two/three-seater, so Bashford cut the roof off and welded up the back doors to make an attractive and streamlined tourer-type body. There was no hood stowage space, so the car had no hood. As originally built, it had a rather upright windscreen, but twin aero screens were substituted later, probably for effect as much as for better aerodynamics. XT1 (Experimental Turbine number 1) is more familiarly known by the name of JET 1, the registration number which the Rover

The third gas turbine car was T2A, with its engine mounted at the rear. The vast exhaust funnel meant that the rear window had to be widened; there were also twin bumpers (purpose unexplained) and an extra air intake ahead of the windscreen. Someone had dented the front passenger door by the time this picture was taken!

Company obtained for it.

After preliminary proving trials before the RAC's Technical Committee in March 1950, at which the world's first turbine car earned its makers the RAC's Dewar Trophy, JET 1 went back to Solihull for further engine development work. It resurfaced over two years later with more power and a new bumperless nose based on the then-current P4 grille, but with Marauder-like front wings. The gas turbine team took it to Belgium, and on June 25, 1952, Spen King achieved a maximum speed of 152.196mph in the car on the sealed-off Jabbeke Highway. More might possibly have been achieved, but as this record-breaking stunt was really for publicity purposes, Rover thought it more profitable to devote the available cash to more practical in-car development work.

A 'more practical' gas turbine car actually existed already. T2, with a much smaller and less powerful power unit installed orthodox-fashion at the front, had already been made from a P4 75 saloon. However, the tremendously hot exhaust gases of the gas turbine engine caused problems; Rover tried to duct them through the chassis side-members, but only extensive and impractical lagging was able to

An unfamiliar shot of JET 1 as first completed, with a convertional windscreen in place of the aero screens with which it was usually seen. Standing behind the car from left to right are Maurice Wilks, Spencer Wilks and Frank Bell, who headed Rover's early gas turbine team.

counter the car's consequent tendency to self-ignite! As a result, T2 was rebuilt as T2A, still under Gordon Bashford's supervision, sometime around 1954. This time the engine went into the boot, and a huge funnel running up to roof height took away the exhaust gases, as well as most of the rearward visibility. It is not quite clear why nothing further came of T2A, although the next gas turbine car, T3, was designed around its power unit, so it may be that the P4 was felt to have reached the limit of its potential as a gas turbine-driven vehicle.

**The Marauder**
No P4 history would be complete without at least a brief look at the Marauder. This two/three-seat sports tourer depended entirely on P4 75 components for its chassis, engine and transmission (although a special overdrive was optionally available, several years before the P4 90 became so equipped), and it depended to no small degree on the same car for its styling. Nevertheless, it was not a Rover product, but was assembled by Wilks, Mackie and Company (later known as the Marauder Car Company) from P4 mechanical parts, and clothed with a body of special design. Between 1950 and the middle of 1952, when increased Purchase Tax priced the Marauder out of the market, 15 were made.

The car was designed by Peter Wilks, George Mackie and Spen King, all Rover employees, with assistance in the styling from Richard Mead, a small Midlands coachbuilder. Their original plan had been to use Rover parts in a traditional cycle-winged open sports car, but the appearance of the Ferrari 166 in 1949 encouraged them to give the car wide-bodied styling based on the P4. A supply of parts from Rover was arranged, Wilks and Mackie left the Rover Company to set up in business making Marauders – though both would later return to Solihull – and the first prototype appeared in July 1950.

Basically, the Marauder used a shortened P4 chassis

Magnificently restored by one of its original designers, George Mackie's Marauder is seen here in 1981. The general resemblance to the P4 body design is clearly seen – and what about those hubcaps and bumpers, and the trim strip at the base of the body!

frame, with a slightly uprated 2,103cc engine mounted further back than in the parent car to avoid its heavy understeer and to give a more appropriate weight distribution. Later, an over-bored engine of 2,390cc, using pistons from the P3 60 and giving 100bhp, would be offered in the Marauder 100, and it would be possible to specify a triple-carburettor option with the larger engine. Only one car of each type was actually built, however.

Marauders were good for around 90mph in basic form, and rather more in '100' form – not exactly road-burners, but certainly sporting and refined for cars of their type. In the early 1950s they established a name for themselves in rallies and even club racing events. A single example was fitted with a rather less sporting fixed-head coupe body to special order, and this, along with at least 10 other Marauders, still survives.

# CHAPTER 4

# A move up-market

## The P5 programme, 1958 – 1973

**P5 3-litre (1958-1967), P5B 3.5-litre (1967-1973), P5 2.4-litre (1962) and 2.6-litre (1962-1966)**

In the early 1950s, Rover's finances favoured an expansion of the model range, and the Company at first toyed with the idea of producing a smaller car than the P4 alongside that model. It soon became clear that neither the capital nor the production facilities then available would stretch to the volume production necessary for such a car, however, and in 1955 a plan was approved to make the new model a bigger car than the P4, a 3-litre luxury saloon which would be produced in relatively small numbers. It would also take Rover into a higher price bracket than they had previously catered for under the Wilks regime.

In common with many other manufacturers, Rover had been experimenting in the early 1950s with monocoque structures, and it was swiftly decided in conjunction with the body stylists that this type of construction offered the opportunity for reducing body height in the search for sleeker lines and better handling without a corresponding loss of interior space. Thus the P5 was drawn up as a monocoque design, with the engine, transmission and front suspension carried on a detachable subframe. Like all the early monocoque cars, it was over-engineered by the time it went into production; stress engineering was then in its infancy, and the solution to all doubts about structural strength was to make the doubtful components thicker! The subframe ended up like a massive part-chassis, and an early experiment with Birmabright alloy body panels was soon aborted in favour of the heavier all-steel construction. It was

thus no mean achievement that the car's overall weight was closely similar to that of the contemporary six-cylinder P4s.

**Mechanical units**

The choice of a 3-litre engine was dictated by the minimum size then considered acceptable in a luxury car rather than for any deeper engineering reasons. A lot of work went into a V6 unit distantly related to the prewar V6 which Jack Swaine had drawn up, but the engine's development was beset by problems, and by late 1955 or early 1956 it had become clear that the V6 could not possibly be ready in time for the P5's projected launch date of 1958. Maurice Wilks instructed Swaine's department to stop work on the engine (which at that stage gave around 100bhp from 2,960cc and was running in several P4 development cars) and to look into the possibility of making a 3-litre unit from the 2,638cc P4 90 block.

It would have been possible simply to over-bore the 90's block and to fit the pistons from a 60, but Swaine's team had lingering doubts about the engine's durability with the resultant thin cylinder walls, so Maurice Wilks revised the requirement, asking for a block of the same dimensions, but with water between all the bores. He also specified a seven-bearing crankshaft (could it have been coincidence that the XK engine in Jaguar's Mk VII saloon already boasted seven main bearings?) to ensure vibration-free running. Norman Bryden, in the Engine Drawing Office, came up with the simple solution of repositioning the cylinder bore centres within the block, as had already been

One of David Bache's earliest proposals for the P5 was this rather chunky-looking machine. Note the rear window design, which had already appeared on the P4.

Viewing of this full-scale mock-up took place on a Sunday morning at Solihull in late 1955. The design now had links with the Farina P4 prototypes, but the wheelbase at this stage was only 108in.

This view of an early P5 Saloon bodyshell shows the massively robust construction.

done once for the 'spread bore' engine, and was able to ensure that the only increase in length was a tiny one, brought about because the water pump impeller now had to move forwards to clear No 1 cylinder barrel. Time and money were saved by using a cylinder head which, as Jack Swaine recalls, was a compromise based on that of the 90. Improved valve gear used roller cam followers (first seen in the 2-litre Land-Rover diesel engine) in place of the pad type, which tended to wear rapidly in the P4 engine; there were a new camshaft, distributor and exhaust manifold, a higher compression ratio and a bigger carburettor, and the 3-litre engine was complete.

From its introduction in the autumn of 1958 until the demise of the Mk IA 3-litre in 1962, the 2,995cc engine developed 115bhp at 4,500rpm. Although this was not significantly more than the 108bhp twin-caburettor P4 engine installed in the 105 models, the torque characteristics of the new engine gave it much greater flexibility over a wider range. Thus the P5 3-litre offered a smoother, more relaxed manner of motoring, as befitted a high-quality

luxury saloon. It was scarcely a quick car, however, and proposals at Board level for 'economy model' P5s – first with a 2-litre 'four' and later with the 2,625cc 'six' – were accordingly given short shrift. The Engineering Department, meanwhile, tried to coax more power from the 3-litre engine by means of various multiple-carburettor systems. The car's relative lack of urge did not go unnoticed outside the Rover Company, either – although, surprisingly, the motoring press never complained in print – and the former racing driver Raymond Mays developed a triple-carburettor installation which he intended to market. Tests made at Solihull, however, showed that the advantages of this installation were minimal, and Mays never actually put his conversion into production.

The Mk I 3-litre engine, produced from 1958 until 1961, used an oil-bath air cleaner, but this was replaced on the 1962 season Mk IA models by an AC paper-element cleaner. This offered easier maintenance and may also have been intended to contribute to better breathing, although the Mk IA engines showed no noticeable power increase over the

The P5 subframe, complete with engine, transmission and front suspension. The rear ends of the subframe side members bolted to the monocoque shell approximately under the front seats. This is an early example, with the original drum brakes.

Mk I variety. Restricted breathing had actually been identified quite early on as the main cause of the 3-litre's lack of power. After the multiple-carburettor experiments, Maurice Wilks asked for simpler ways of improving the engine's breathing, and the engine development team eventually came up with the so-called 'Weslake head', which has already been described in Chapter 3.

Solihull's original plan had been to fit a high-performance version of the 3-litre engine to the forthcoming Coupe models, but in the event, the 'Weslake head' engine was fitted to both Saloon and Coupe Mk II 3-litre models in autumn 1962. As fitted to manual-transmission cars, it offered 134bhp and a slight increase in maximum torque,

both at higher crankshaft speeds than in the Mk I version. A lower-compression version with other minor differences and developing 129bhp was fitted to automatic cars, as their transmission required different torque characteristics, and a less tortuous exhaust system on both manual and automatic Mk II models released a little more of this new-found power to the road wheels. If the automatics were still rather deficient in acceleration, they could at least top the 100mph mark without difficulty, and the manual transmission Mk IIs could boast a performance worthy of such a large engine. By this time, however, the rather sedate market into which the 3-litre had been launched was beginning to change, and there were signs that many customers at the top end of the market were now prepared to sacrifice a little luxury for a lot more performance. Although the car continued to sell well, it never repeated the sales success of its first years, and settled down as a steady seller in a rapidly shrinking market.

From autumn 1964, the 3-litre engine was given larger main bearing journals to counteract a torsional vibration of the crankshaft which Solihull's engineers had encountered with the 'Weslake head' engine. No normal owner would ever have detected this, but the story does demonstrate how much attention to detail went into Rover development! Cars fitted with this engine were designated Mk IIC models. The same engine, with its accompanying larger-capacity cooling system, also powered the facelifted Mk III models introduced for the 1966 season, when a change in the type of automatic transmission led to the 134bhp engine being fitted to automatic as well as manual-gearbox Mk IIIs, but otherwise there were no major changes of specification.

With the introduction of the 3.5-litre model in 1967, Rover were at last able to provide the sort of performance which the luxury market was by now demanding. By this stage, of course, the car's body design was beginning to date, but that seems to have worked in its favour, allowing the new model to carve out a niche in the market which was all its own. The 3.5-litre was powered by a lightweight all-alloy 3,528cc V8 engine which had been developed from a General Motors design, and was related to the engines with which Jack Brabham and his team had won world motor racing titles in 1966 and 1967.

The story of the V8 has been told many times, but bears repetition. Managing Director William Martin-Hurst spotted one of the GM engines in 1963 while on a visit to Mercury Marine, at Fond du Lac, Wisconsin, to sell Rover engines for marine applications. On inquiring of that company's Carl Keikhaefer what it was, he learned that it had been taken out of a Buick and was intended for experimental use in a powerboat. He was staggered to learn that the engine had actually ceased production after only three years, when the American motoring public had turned its back on the 'compact' cars of the early 1960s. Measurements showed that it was just the right size to fit into the engine bays of both the P5 and the P6, and Martin-Hurst says now that he knew

The ex-General Motors V8 engine in P5B form.

right away he just had to have that engine for Rover. By 1964 it was being examined in Solihull; the Rover Company gained a licence to manufacture it in January 1965, and it went into production at Solihull as soon as was humanly possible after that.

The General Motors '215' (it displaced 215 cubic inches) had first appeared in autumn 1960 in the 1961 season 'compact' cars – the Buick Special, Pontiac Tempest and Oldsmobile F-85 Cutlass. In Buick and Pontiac form, it breathed through a twin-choke Rochester carburettor to give 155bhp at 4,600rpm and 220lb/ft of torque at 2,400rpm, while the Oldsmobile variety had different pistons and cylinder heads and a higher power output. All varieties were die-cast from a strong but lightweight aluminium alloy, and all had hydraulic self-adjusting tappets to promote quiet running.

Rover retained the engine's basic dimensions and layout,

but made a number of other modifications. Instead of die-casting the blocks with the cylinder liners held in place, they went for sand-casting with press-fit liners. Breathing was improved to give a slightly higher rev range, and a new inlet manifold was designed to take twin SU carburettors in place of the Rochester. A manual choke control replaced the typically American automatic choke, and the compression ratio was raised to 10.5:1 to give a maximum power output of 184bhp at 5,200rpm and a torque figure of 226lb/ft at 3,000rpm. Those who worked at Solihull have commented that the degree of change wrought by Rover engineers on the American design is too often understated; that is probably true, but it should also be said that Rover would never have got to grips with an American V8 so quickly if they had not imported Joe Turley, Buick's chief engine designer, along with the engine. Turley, who was almost due to retire from GM, was delighted to help in the further development of what was, after all, one of 'his' engines.

The V8 weighed-in at 200lb less than Rover's faithful IOE 'six', so it took out the weight as well as putting in the power. Weight distribution changed as well, the new model being less nose-heavy than the superseded one, and consequently it handled rather better despite some complaints that the lighter front end removed all traces of feel from the power steering. Although the P5B (B for the Buick engine) was no sports car, and was limited to a 115mph top speed because of the gearing which went with its automatic transmission, it could comfortably out-accelerate even the relatively quick manual-transmission 3-litre, and its fuel consumption was actually better than the superseded model's (though, in fairness, overdrive 3-litres were still more economical on long runs). That the P5 'chassis' design accepted all these extra strains and stresses without protest is an indication of the soundness of its basic concept.

There were no major revisions to the P5B engine before the model went out of production in the summer of 1973. From the beginning, it had an alternator instead of the 3-litre's dynamo, and the power-steering pump, dynamo-driven on the older model, became belt-driven direct from the crankshaft pulley. The first V8s wore rocker shafts very quickly, and the shaft material was changed quite early on. An automatic choke was fitted in 1968 (Rover called it an Automatic Enrichment Device or AED for short), but its reputation was destroyed partly because supply difficulties forced the factory to fit a number of cars with manual choke

The chrome strip above the rear number-plate was echoed on P4s after 1958. This is a Mk IA, with underlined marque name on the boot lid and no '3 litre' badging. The chromed fuel filler lid persisted until 1963. Photographed by Alan Milstead.

controls, and partly because the device itself was never as reliable as Solihull would have liked. By 1974 Rover were shamefacedly offering a conversion kit to manual choke, and probably a high proportion of automatic chokes were replaced by frustrated owners.

Three different transmission options were available on the Mk I 3-litre cars: four-speed manual, four-speed manual with overdrive, and automatic. The automatic and non-overdrive cars shared a 3.9:1 axle ratio, while 4.3:1 was specified with the overdrive. Manual gearboxes were identical to the contemporary P4 items, with synchromesh on the three upper ratios, and the overdrive was the P4's Laycock DeNormanville unit with electrical control and a kickdown switch beneath the accelerator pedal. The gear lever of these early 3-litres was the familiar 'pot-stirrer' type also inherited from the P4.

Although the Roverdrive automatic transmission of the 105R had been tried during P5 development, it was found to overheat when installed behind the 3-litre engine, and so the automatic 3-litre had a Borg-Warner type DG box, a

Looking altogether more purposeful than the Mk I is this Mk II 3-litre Saloon. Most of the exterior cosmetic changes had been introduced on the Mk IA models, but Mk IIs rode an inch lower on their suspension than earlier cars.

The 3-litre Coupe first appeared in Mk II form for the 1963 season. Two-tone arrangements differed from those of Saloons.

three-speed unit which was also used in contemporary Jaguars. This remained on the 3-litre's option list until the introduction of the Mk III models in autumn 1965, the only modifications coming with the Mk IA models, which had an adjustable electrically-operated intermediate gear hold in place of the earlier cable-operated control. The new control also permitted selection of bottom gear when starting from rest; shortly after the 3-litre's introduction, the automatic models had been modified to give a 'second speed start', a refinement introduced to give a smoother takeoff by eliminating one of the upward changes.

The non-overdrive cars were discontinued with the arrival of the 1961 season Mk Is, but changes to the manual gearbox itself had to wait until the introduction of the Mk II models the following year. These cars and the Mk IIIs which followed had raised second and third gear ratios,

which gave a closer-spaced set of ratios and improved acceleration. The overdrive kickdown facility was discontinued because its use at the higher speeds of which these cars were capable could have caused overspeeding of the engine and unpleasant transmission snatch. Perhaps most important from the driver's point of view, the close-ratio gearbox was operated by a short remote-control gear lever sited on the transmission tunnel, which gave more precise selection than the infamous 'pot-stirrer', and incorporated as an additional refinement a pushbutton detent protecting reverse.

From autumn 1965, all automatics (special-order Mk IIs excepted) used the Borg-Warner type 35 gearbox, an improved unit of greater torque capacity offering smoother changes. This transmission had actually been tested in the V8 development programme when that engine had proved

A Mk III 3-litre Saloon. Principal external differences from earlier cars were the thicker trim strip and larger grille badge, together with 'Mk III' badging.

The 3.5-litre Coupe remains the most sought-after variant of the P5. This early two-tone car belonged to Rover's press fleet. Badging remained unchanged until the end of production, despite the redesignation of cars as 3½-litre models in autumn 1968.

too much for the DG box (a type 8 had also proved unsatisfactory), and it was not until then that its potential advantages for the 3-litre had become apparent. It permitted use of the 134bhp engine, which the DG box had not; it could be dropped from the car for servicing independently of the engine and subframe, which the DG box could not; and with new internal ratios combined with a 3.54:1 axle it gave acceleration which required fewer engine revolutions for the same effect and was consequently both quieter and (marginally) more economical. On Mk III models it was accompanied by an oil cooler fitted ahead of the radiator, and Rover took care to provide a long filler tube which emerged under the bonnet so that it was no longer necessary to remove the carpets to check the fluid level. Mk III automatics also had a different selector quadrant, which read PRNDL instead of the PNDLR of the DG-transmission cars, the changed reverse position being one of the earliest effects on Rover of American safety legislation.

A rather special 3.5-litre Saloon built for Prime Minister Harold Wilson in 1967. The apparently standard exterior belies the wealth of special features fitted to the car.

The 3-litre's manual gearbox – which dated in essence from the 1934 Rovers – was unable to cope with the V8's torque, and Rover had no other suitable unit available. The 3.5-litre cars, therefore, went into production with the automatic transmission as standard, and as Rover's Sales Division were convinced that a manual gearbox was not necessary in the big luxury saloon market, the car was never offered with anything other than the type 35 transmission. The 3-litre automatics had had their transmission selector on the steering column, but from the beginning of V8 production the selector was located on the centre console. For the first year of production, the 3.5-litres had an L-D1-D2 selector, but with the series B models for 1969 came both higher change-up speed settings and a 1-2-D selector range which gave a greater degree of manual override control but no longer permitted the smooth (and fuel-saving) second-speed start. There were no further transmission changes before P5B production was terminated.

The constant process of detail improvement which marked the P5's career was visible also in the braking and steering

revisions introduced over the years. The first cars had a servo-assisted all-drum braking system generally similar to that of the P4 90 and 105, but from autumn 1959 Girling disc brakes were fitted to the front wheels. This was in response to market pressure rather than because the drum brakes were in any way inadequate, although it is probably true to say that some changes would have been necessary to cope with the increased speed of the Mk II models if the disc brakes had not already been specified. Later Mk Is and all Mk IAs had a vacuum reservoir tank for the servo, but Mk IIs and Mk IIIs did not. There were no more changes of note until the V8-engined models had a Lockheed servo instead of the original Girling type, together with harder disc pads to cope with the higher performance; the vacuum reservoir tank returned with this installation. From the beginning, the handbrake was a pull-out lever by the driver's outboard hand under the facia and, despite minor revisions to the linkage over the years, it was never one of the car's better points. As for steering, the Burman recirculating ball unit was supplemented from autumn 1959

Facia of a Mk I Automatic. The T-handle beside the cigar lighter was a highly inaccessible intermediate gear hold. Later models would differ considerably from the first production cars, even though the general layout of instruments and controls did not alter.

by an optional Hydrasteer variable-ratio power-assisted system, the first powered system on a production Rover. This was standard on all Coupes, and was then standardized on Mk IIC and later Saloons as well. The only significant change was in the pump drive already discussed, which came with the V8-engined models.

The P5's power-assisted steering has often been criticized for being too light, and for transmitting too little feel of the road to the driver. Certainly, the Hydrasteer system was primitive by later standards, but in the hands of a sensitive driver it gave no cause for worry. By contrast, the non-assisted steering of the first cars was considered too heavy, particularly at parking speeds, and Mk II Saloons were given a higher-geared steering box for the 1964 season, to become Mk IIB models (the 'B' suffix denoted the steering change; as all Coupes had PAS, they remained unchanged and retained the Mk IIA designation). At the same time, the hydraulic damper employed with manual

steering was changed for a friction-type damper, which was perhaps cheaper but was neither adjustable nor serviceable.

Throughout the P5's life, suspension was by semi-elliptic variable-rate leaf springs at the rear, with laminated torsion bars for the independently-sprung front wheels. From the Mk II onwards, the ride height was reduced by an inch to give better handling properties. Certain export markets were supplied with cars which had heavy-duty rear springs (Rover called them 'high suspension' springs), and an 'H' stamped on the commission number plate identified these cars. All the cars were delivered with crossply tyres, normally of 6.70 section, although an option discontinued when the Mk IAs arrived was 7.10-section tyres. On the electrical side, a positive-earth system was used until the demise of the Mk IIs, when negative-earth electrics were introduced as part of a policy to permit the use of standard transistorized electrical components across the range.

There were two special export-only variants of the P5,

The interior of Mk I Saloons dated very quickly. This is one of the very first, with the original transverse pleating on the seats.

which were the first Rovers (simple LHD conversions apart) built exclusively for the export market. In both cases, smaller engines were fitted to circumvent penal tax jumps in the territories to which the cars were exported. Thus, from about spring 1962, France and Nigeria were offered a P5 model fitted with the 2,625cc 'Weslake head' engine of the P4 110 – the very model which had earlier been under consideration as an economy model for the home market. The 2.6-litre, as it was called, was identical in every way except for its engine and badging to the contemporary 3-litre Saloon; it first appeared in Mk IA guise and it ceased production as a Mk II in 1966. Sales were never high, despite the production of both LHD and RHD versions,

and of course acceleration and maximum speed were closer to those of Mk I 3-litres. Throughout its life, the 2.6-litre retained the P4-type wide-ratio gearbox of the Mk I/IA cars, which was better suited to its torque characteristics but, of course, detracted from all-out acceleration; there was never an automatic option. Even rarer – and slower – was the 2.4-litre model sold in Austria. No doubt the short-stroke IOE 'six' of 2,445cc had been developed with something else in mind, as it is inconceivable that it should have been built solely for a limited overseas market in one model. The story goes, however, that Rover's Austrian importers thought they could sell a 2.4-litre P5 in sensible quantities, and more or less badgered Solihull into making one. However, sales were very poor indeed, and the model was available for only a short time (roughly spring to summer 1962), while the engine was never used in another production Rover. Like the 2.6-litre, the car used the wide-ratio gearbox and was offered only with manual transmission; otherwise, it was identical to the contemporary 3-litre Saloons.

**Bodies**

The P5 body was styled by David Bache, working under Maurice Wilks' guidance. As usual, Wilks started with a pre-existing body shape – in this case that of the Farina fixed-head coupe on the P4 90 chassis – and adapted it. As Bache was a trained stylist, the finished product perhaps reflected as many of his ideas as of Wilks', but he has commented that it was not easy in those days to get his own way! The original design was for a four-light saloon, but once its basic shape had been established, Wilks asked his body team (the mid-1950s saw the creation of a Styling Department at Solihull for the first time) to draw up what was variously called a 'Sports Saloon', a 'Hard Top', or a '3-litre S' variant. Several designs were proposed, but the one eventually chosen for production simply added a lower roof and more steeply raked front and rear screens to the same lower body hull. As originally conceived, it had frameless side windows like the contemporary Mercedes-Benz coupes, but problems with these, plus the huge cost of tooling up for production, meant that only the Saloon version was approved for 1958 introduction; the 'Sports Saloon' body style was shelved and would not be made available until 1962.

In designing the P5's body, Rover tried to avoid the pitfalls of the P4 design. Thus the petrol tank was placed between the boot and the rear seat so that the boot floor was level and unobstructed; the spare wheel again lived in a tray beneath the boot floor, but this time the tray wound down to permit access; and the rear wing panels were bolted rather than welded to the main body structure, thus ensuring cheaper and easier accident repairs.

The production Saloon body relied for its effect on simple styling set off by subtly positioned trim lines. This was the classic Bache approach. Where the Farina body had hinted

It is difficult to see from this publicity shot of a Mk II Coupe interior how restricted was the rear leg room. Door trims, seats and gearbox tunnel carpeting have all changed from the Mk I/IA cars, and their general pattern was echoed on Saloon models, although this type of wood trim on the doors was a Coupe peculiarity.

at separate wings in its rear body side pressings, Bache's slab-sided P5 was relieved only by a slim chromed strip which terminated in a neat downturn over the front wheelarch. Badging was almost entirely absent, with only the 'Rover' name on the boot lid and a discreet 'Rover 3-litre' badge on the top bar of the wide radiator grille, which echoed the Farina design. There were no quarter-lights, but perspex louvres over the side windows, recalling the Rovers of the 1930s, were designed to give draught-free ventilation; as it turned out, they also created wind roar at speed and distorted vision! New hubcaps with a stylized Rover emblem recessed into the centre differed from the P4 pattern, and the body was longer, lower and wider than the P4, although there was a deliberate overall similarity, particularly in the car's frontal aspect.

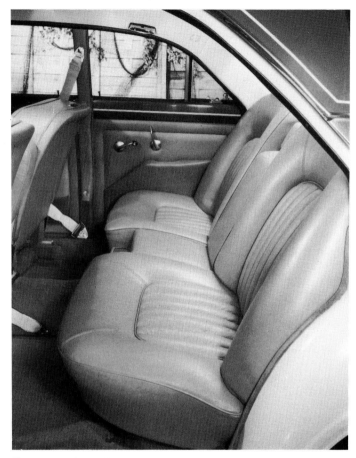

The seats of the Mk III and P5B models were eventually based on those designed for the 2000, although a more distinctive design had been tried experimentally.

The Mk I bodies had an attractive interior design, in which charcoal grey panels and instrument surround set off the main colour. The dashboard and door cappings were polished wood, while the seats had padded edge rolls with pleating running across the centre panels. Either a bench seat or two individual seats could be had at the front. Deep pile carpets were fitted, but the headlining was plastic, like that introduced shortly before on P4 models. Although the passenger compartment really was longer than the P4's, an illusion of even greater space was created by setting the facia panel well forward; the glove boxes were shallower, but a parcel shelf running across the front at knee height compensated for the loss. Padded rolls all round indicated the first stirrings of Rover's interest in passive safety features, and the new pod-style instrument panel carried another 'first' in a Rover – a key-activated starter switch.

The original interior design had trim-coloured padding around the window frames, but this was changed in autumn 1960 when the wooden door cappings were extended all round the windows in the P4 manner. The transverse seat pleating was replaced by pleating running from front to back, and there were also changes to the headlining, the interior mirror, the air vents in the facia and the rear

It was possible to specify head restraints for the front seats of Mk IIIs and P5Bs, complete with a rear passenger's reading light.

A rarity is the Radford division, which was available for the 3-litre Saloons prior to the Mk III.

courtesy lights, while automatic models had a new red 'handbrake on' warning light. The 1961 models all had stainless steel exterior trim in place of chrome-plated brass, and there was a small change to the fillet over the front wheelarch.

The P5 had always been intended to appeal to the chauffeur-drive market, and for the 1961 season the Radford coachbuilding concern introduced a detachable limousine division similar to that which they also marketed for the contemporary Rolls-Royce and Bentley models. This was a rather expensive extra, however, and probably no more than half a dozen were made before it was withdrawn in 1967; none are known to survive, although a single example of a similar division of unknown make survives on a 1969 model 3.5-litre Saloon.

Although there were important mechanical changes over the next four seasons, the alterations to body and interior were almost wholly cosmetic. The two-tone interior which had appeared so chic in the late 'fifties had dated quickly, and the grey contrast panels were deleted with the arrival of the Mk II models for the 1963 season. At the same time, there were new front armrests and the steering column/instrument panel assembly changed to black. Neater stainless steel trim appeared on the interior woodwork, and the window winder handles gained black plastic grips.

Fully-adjustable individual front seats had arrived as an option shortly after the autumn 1961 introduction of Mk IA models, and the repositioned gear lever on manual-transmission Mk II models meant that these cars had to have individual front seats of one sort or the other; on the automatics, the bench seat in fact became less common as time went on.

From the inside, Mk IIs were also distinguished from Mk IAs by clearer faces to the instruments, spade-shaped switches and a larger amber handbrake warning light (the red light had been standardized for both manual and automatic transmission on Mk IA cars), while Mk IIC models could be spotted by the revised switchgear occasioned by the introduction of twin-speed windscreen wipers, and by a pointer instead of a ring on the automatic transmission selector panel. Safety belts, which were first offered on Mk IAs, were not standardized until much later, although they were almost invariably fitted to the front seats of Mk II cars.

Colours and trim changed for Mk II production, but then remained constant until autumn 1966, and although Mk IAs could be distinguished from Mk Is by their larger stainless steel wheel trims, the presence of front quarter-lights and the absence of louvres over the side windows, Mk IIs were less easy to tell from Mk IAs. The keen-eyed would have

The Pressed Steel estate car conversion suffered from body rigidity problems and would have cost nearly twice as much as the standard Saloon if it had gone into production.

noticed a new grille badge and altered badging on the boot lid, while later Mk IIs could be identified by the painted fuel filler cap which replaced the chrome type during Mk IIB production in 1963. A number of the later cars were also fitted with Webasto's fabric sunroof, which became an approved extra for 1964.

The launch of the Mk III 3-litres was almost certainly brought forward as a sales ploy to revive interest in the car before the introduction of the V8-engined model, as the Mk II models remained available alongside them for a year (at a slightly lower cost), doubtless in an attempt to use up stocks of old parts. Changes to the outside of the Mk IIIs were restricted to new badging on the grille and boot lid, with 'Mk III' badges adorning the latter and the front wings. A thicker side trim strip was added, without the neat downturn over the front wheelarch, and it terminated in three symbolic pips on the rear wings. In addition, a new circular chromed petrol filler cap was fitted. Although two-tone Saloons were available during the 1966 season, the new style did not lend itself very well to this treatment, and

most cars were ordered in a single colour. When the colour options were revised for 1967, single colours were standardized on Saloons.

Just as the new grille badge was P6-derived (probably to create some kind of family unity between the two widely different ranges), so the new seats were a larger version of the lightweight P6 design. Their heavily padded edges gave much improved support, and adjustable front headrests with built-in reading lamps for rear passengers were offered as an optional extra. Saloon models could be supplied with either a rear seat split into two individual units, P6-fashion, or a traditional bench seat; but bench front seats were no longer available, and all individual front seats were now fully-adjustable. Rear headrests could also be specified for Saloons. There was a rear heater, with a fan operated from a switch panel on the transmission tunnel, and a new rear parcel shelf in the interior colour contained provision for an additional radio speaker, which could be controlled from a switch adjacent to the rear heater fan control. A steel reinforcing edge reappeared on the front parcel shelf, having been absent throughout Mk II production, and a 'modesty skirt' now shrouded the handbrake warning light. At the front, the tool tray was moved to the centre and given a veneer lid so that it doubled as a picnic tray; rear seat passengers had their own foldaway picnic tray concealed behind the armrest, as well as a trinket box between the seats on four-seater Saloon models. Detail revisions included the repositioning of the clock to the passenger's side corner fillet of the facia, where it now had a black bezel, and the loss of both map pockets and ashtrays from the front seat backs, the latter being recessed into the armrests on Saloon models. In addition, maximum gear speeds were marked on the speedometer in automatic Saloons.

If the Mk III 3-litres had represented a sort of 'halfway-house' between the Mk IIs and the 3.5-litre models, there was no mistaking the P5Bs when they were introduced in 1968. Instant recognition points were the fog lights sunk into the front wings below the headlamps, the chromed Rostyle wheels and the rubber-faced overriders. Less immediately obvious were a new gilded metal grille badge, the absence of the starting-handle support from the front number-plate box, and wider spacing of the Rover name on the boot lid. The side trim lost its three pips, and now contained repeater flashers on front and rear wings, while there was an additional strip on the body sill, which was painted matt black in an attempt to slim down the side elevation; '3.5-litre' plate badges on front wings and boot lid, and a twin-barrelled exhaust tailpipe completed the transformation. There were to be no more external changes to the cars, although Sundym tinted glass became an option in 1969 and a Triplex Hotline heated rear window with yellow elements replaced the laminated type with concealed elements in 1971.

The V8-engined cars retained the Mk III 3-litre's interior, but with some small changes. A new console was constructed on the gearbox hump and carried the gear selector lever, an ashtray (displacing the plastic ones under the parcel shelf), and the cigar lighter and switch for the fog lights. The switch for the heated rear window was installed alongside when, as was almost invariably the case, that option was fitted to the car. There was additionally a small tray for trinkets ahead of the selector lever. Carpet colours were now limited to grey or beige, depending on seat colours. Next to the choke control was a T-handle for the petrol reserve control, which was now a mechanical component as there was a single fuel pump in place of the twin pumps of the 3-litre. The only other notable change was the loss of the oil level indicator switch which had been

This 3-litre drophead by FLM Panelcraft was made for a private customer and cost about £700, or around half the price of the car when new. Huge reinforcing irons were fitted beneath the trim strip on the body sills.

found on every other Rover (P4 80 and P6 models excepted) built under the Wilks regime.

Subsequent changes were all minor. A larger rear-view mirror was specified from March 1968, and from that autumn the gear lever knob had a cutaway centre, while the front ashtray gained a plain instead of a ribbed lid. Thinner front seat squabs also gave additional legroom in the rear. When the automatic choke was fitted (December 1968 on Coupes, February 1969 on Saloons), the choke control and warning light were both deleted. In January 1971, a thiefproof ignition lock was fitted and the keylock moved to a steering column position; at the same time, inertia-reel front seat belts were standardized, a modification to the B/C posts made in October 1969 having first permitted their fitting. An incidental change was that the P5Bs were renamed 3½-litres from autumn 1968 in an attempt to avoid confusion with the then new P6B 3500. Badging, however, was never altered.

Coupe bodies were introduced with the Mk II models for 1963, and in general they followed the same development as their Saloon counterparts; like these, they were built by the Pressed Steel Company at Swindon. They were readily recognizable by their lower roofline and raked front and rear screens; there was also a decorative stainless-steel plate on the rear quarter-pillars and a 'Coupe' badge on the boot lid. Only fully-adjustable individual front seats were available, while the rear seats were lower and set further forward than in Saloons in order to compensate for a loss of rear headroom. Right from the beginning of Coupe production the rear seats were fitted out as two individual units, and their central panel contained a 'smoker's companion' consisting of a cigar lighter and ashtray. The wooden door cappings were deeper than those of Saloon models and did not continue around the window frames, which on Coupes were of stainless steel. Sill buttons for the door locks were provided, and all Coupes had the rear parcel shelf in the interior trim colour. The only other differences were in instrumentation; a rev-counter replaced the Saloon's com-bined instruments dial, and the three displaced gauges were matched by an oil pressure gauge and mounted in twin binnacles under the main instrument pod. Two-tone Coupes were available until the end of P5B production and differed from two-tone Saloons by having the roof in one colour while the whole lower hull was in the second.

Not surprisingly, the P5's monocoque construction deterred the private coachbuilders from offering alternative body styles. Nevertheless, a few special-bodied cars were built. The earliest of these was an estate variant, converted from a 1959 Mk I Saloon by Pressed Steel, allegedly with the aim of demonstrating to the Rover Company that the 3-litre could rival the contemporary Humber estate cars. The car was evaluated at Solihull and the single prototype (some say that two were made) returned to Pressed Steel. The Rover Company themselves next commissioned a two-door drop-head prototype from the Parisian coachbuilder Chapron. The conversion was carried out in 1961 on an earlier Mk I Saloon, but it was evaluated in France by the Company's representatives and appears never to have come back to the UK. It is believed to have gone to a buyer in Switzerland, and so may well have inspired the Zurich coachbuilder Graber to construct a two-door convertible out of a left-hand-drive Saloon, which he then exhibited at the 1963 Geneva Motor Show. Several Solihull employees recall seeing a Farina-bodied 3-litre convertible, basically similar to the Farina P4 drophead, although their sightings lack documentary or photographic confirmation, and three more unconfirmed drophead 3-litres are said to have been built in the early 1960s by a firm in Feltham, Middlesex. The last known drophead 3-litre was built in 1964 for a private customer by FLM Panelcraft, of London, whose two-door conversion featured a four-light hood, unlike the other known cars, which were two-light designs. This latter car, which was also evaluated at Solihull, was last heard of in the West Country in the late 1970s. As for the others, all have disappeared except for the Graber drophead, which still survives in Switzerland.

# CHAPTER 5

# A Rover for the new generation

## The P6 image-changer, 1963 – 1977

**P6 2000 (1963-1973), 2000TC and Automatic (1966-1973), 2200SC, TC and Automatic (1973-1976); P6B 3500 (1968-1976) and 3500S (1971-1976); North American P6B 3500S (1969-1971)**

Rover changed a lot in the 1950s. For a start, the prosperity brought by the Land-Rover meant that the Company could afford to be more ambitious and adventurous, and Maurice Wilk's engagement of David Bache had an outward sign of Rover's awareness that there were valid new ideas coming from a younger generation of engineers which could and should go into the Company's products. Solihull itself already had two brilliant young engineers on its staff in the shape of Peter Wilks and Spen King, and even before Maurice Wilks ceded his position as Chief Engineer to Robert Boyle in 1956, it had been decided that the 'younger generation' should be given its head. With Spencer and Maurice Wilks still in overall control, at least any radical new ideas would be very carefully scrutinized!

It would be wrong, however, to see in this a sudden change of heart in Rover's management. The fact was that the market was changing in the mid-1950s, and if Rover were to survive they had to respond to these changes. The British car market was becoming much less parochial and consequently more receptive to engineering innovation. Just as British cars had to compete with foreign (mostly European) products abroad, so they were now having to fight an increasing number of these cars on their home ground. The new cars were opening up new market sectors, but at the same time restricting old ones; the up-and-coming

executive no longer wanted a pale imitation of his boss' Rover 90, as Solihull found when they tried to sell the P4 60. He wanted a smart, rapid and practical car which reflected his own smartness, alertness and practicality. Yet he did not want to lose touch altogether with the wood-and-leather of the boardroom and his boss' car. So the P6 was conceived with two priorities in mind which were wholly new to Rover – the export market and the 'young executive' sector. At the same time, it had to be recognizably a Rover. That Solihull succeeded so well in all these design aims is demonstrated by the ambivalent reactions which the car has always provoked among Rover enthusiasts – many complain that it did not have enough of the Rover tradition in it, while others claim that it completely outshone any of its predecessors! Rover laughed all the way to the bank.

The P6 really materialized out of a series of 'ideas sessions' held in Robert Boyle's office. The agenda was rather loosely defined as discussions on a replacement model for the P4, and all kinds of weird and wonderful schemes – flat-four engines, rear engines, hydropneumatic suspension, front-wheel drive and so on – were proposed before some measure of agreement was reached in October 1957. Preliminary mockup and layout work was completed by the end of that year, and a firm specification was issued on New Year's Day 1958.

The specification of a lightweight saloon with a 103in wheelbase, built on a base-unit structure, was inherited from the original P5 proposals of 1953, when that car had been

P6/1, the first 2000 running prototype, is seen here on test during March 1959. It has the original shark nose and pillarless cabin design. The woollen tufts attached to the body were used to study air flow.

projected as a smaller car than the P4. The P6 was to be a four-seater with an engine of between 1,800cc and 2,000cc, capable of 100mph and giving better fuel economy than the P4 without loss of the traditional Rover qualities of durability, reliability and ride comfort. Considering that the P4 105S had only just become the first production Rover to attain 100mph, and that from 2.6 litres, this was a pretty tall order. The programme scheduled the launch of the new car for October 1961, which made that order even taller!

As things were to turn out, the P6 was granted an extra two years' development time. Rover realized that in order to build it they needed a new factory, space for which was readily available on the Solihull site. Building permission was not forthcoming from the Government of the day, however, whose employment policy was to create new jobs in depressed areas, not to attract more labour to the already populous West Midlands. Eventually, a bargain was struck in the autumn of 1960: Rover could build a new assembly block at Solihull provided they also built a new factory at Pengam, near Cardiff, for component manufacture. There

was now no chance that the P6 would be in production on schedule, and it was to be October 1963 before it actually appeared as the new Rover 2000 in the showrooms. Sadly, the P6 was the last Rover with which Maurice Wilks would be associated; he died a few weeks before it was revealed to the public.

**Base and mechanical units**

The base-unit structure of the P6 was hardly revolutionary, as some writers have suggested: Citroën relied on it for the DS models introduced in 1954, one of which was purchased by Rover in 1958 for examination. Nevertheless, it was an unusual method of construction, and for a company with an image as conservative as Rover's it represented a radically new departure. The P6 base-unit was in effect a steel skeleton which formed both the body-frame and the 'chassis'. All mechanical components were attached to it, and the P6 'skeleton' could be driven as a complete unit; indeed, all completed base-units were road-tested in this condition before the body panels were bolted into place.

Before letting the P6 prototypes loose on the roads, Rover disguised them with 'Talago' badges, and even set up a Talago Motor Company so that the name on the tax disc would not give the game away! The name came from the initials of T.L. Gawronski, who was P6 Project Engineer. Photograph by Alan Milstead; badge from the Geoff Kent Collection.

Although the base-unit was largely Robert Boyle's baby, chassis engineering was contributed by Gordon Bashford, who centred his whole concept of the car's ride and handling on the use of radial-ply tyres, which had never before been seen on a Rover. At the rear, he specified a sliding-joint De Dion set up with location by Watts linkages and fixed-length drive shafts, which gave most of the advantages of independent rear suspension without its complexity; it also pleased Spen King and Peter Wilks, who favoured such a layout after their experiences with the Rover Special racing car (see Chapter 7). Braking was by power-assisted discs on all four wheels, inboard at the rear to reduce unsprung weight, and there was Adamant hour-glass worm-and-roller steering. The front suspension was an odd design, with horizontal coil springs transferring the stresses to the front bulkhead; partly, it was conceived in order to leave a very

wide engine bay, as a gas turbine-powered P6 was under consideration for eventual production and its power unit was rather bulky. In the event, only a single prototype (T4) was built, but the wide engine bay was to prove a boon later when larger-engined P6s were developed.

The engine of the Rover 2000 was a completely new overhead-camshaft four-cylinder unit of 'square' dimensions, which displaced 1,978cc and put out 90bhp when installed. To keep height down in order to get the engine under the car's low bonnet, a Heron-head 'bowl-in-piston' design was used. The Company's Sales Division, in fact, had been strongly opposed to the idea of a four-cylinder engine from the beginning as they had never had much success with the four-cylinder P4 60, and Maurice Wilks had had severe reservations at first about using an overhead camshaft, which he thought would be noisy. To be honest, the 2000's engine was never anywhere near as quiet and refined as the IOE

The gas turbine T4 was made from the 10th prototype P6 (P6/10). When it appeared, in 1961, the public could not have known that it embodied most of the shape of the forthcoming new Rover. Although small changes have been made over the years, the extended shovel-nose remains substantially as it was originally built.

The P6's base-unit. The idea had been seen before in the Citroen DS 19, but Rover had been toying with this method of construction in 1953, over a year before the Citroen was launched.

units of the P3s, P4s and P5s, but for a large four-cylinder it was certainly above contemporary standards. Although there had been all kinds of problems during development, the free-revving, lusty little engine which went into production was able to haul the car beyond its 100mph design target when required. Like all Rover engines built under the Wilks regime, it soon acquired a reputation for longevity and reliability – and this time for fuel economy, too. Its frugal petrol consumption enabled Rover to avoid the additional cost of an overdrive (although one was later tried experimentally), and the 2000 had nothing more complicated than a four-speed all-synchromesh gearbox, designed specifically for it and mated to a fairly high final drive of 3.54:1. The well-chosen ratios of the gearbox meant that acceleration was always available when required, and despite a rather notchy change mechanism, the remote-control gear lever actively encouraged the driver to make use of his gearbox.

Right from the design stage, Solihull's engineers had tried to build safety into the 2000, an aim which was almost unique in the late 1950s. Everything possible was done to make the car both actively safe (to avoid accidents) and passively safe (to protect the occupants if they were involved in one), and the Rover 2000 was awarded the AA's Gold Medal in 1965 for its outstanding contribution to safer motoring. Safe did not mean boring, however, and the car's superb roadholding, excellent gearbox and first-class brakes and steering made it a driver's car quite unlike previous Rovers, with an appeal way beyond the traditional Rover market. Triumph's rival 2000, launched shortly afterwards, was positively agricultural in comparison. Contemporary road-testers went into ecstasies when they first got their hands on a P6, but several of them pointed out that the car's chassis design was too good for its engine and that the P6 literally cried out for more power.

To be fair to Rover, this became abundantly apparent to

them during the car's development. A gas turbine option might have fitted the bill, but it was still a long way off, and in any case it looked like being expensive. What was wanted was a more powerful petrol engine, and quickly. The IOE engines were too tall and too heavy, so in 1962 Jack Swaine's department started work on a six-cylinder variant of the 2000 engine, which used the same bore and stroke to arrive at a swept volume of 2,967cc. This certainly put in the power, but it was also half as long again as the 'four', and installation involved lengthening the front end of the car, which entailed major alterations to the base-unit as well as new panelling. The car was going to be so different with

this engine that it was given its own designation of P7.

Although Solihull seriously considered putting it into production, the P7 promised to be expensive in terms of new body tooling, so Robert Boyle suggested in 1964 that it might be worthwhile looking into a 2½-litre five-cylinder engine based on the 'four', which would have the advantage that it could just be squeezed into the existing P6 engine bay. Five-cylinder car engines were unheard-of in those days of course, although five-cylinder diesel engines for commercial vehicles had existed for some time, and Rover's engine designers set to with enthusiasm. They were working on problems of in-car balance for the 2,472cc units which were

The De Dion rear end gave exceptionally good roadholding, and ride comfort better than that of any Rover before or since. Changing pads on the inboard disc brakes was not to be the easiest of jobs, however.

running at the end of 1964, when both the five-cylinder engine and the P7 project were cancelled in favour of the 3½-litre V8 which Managing Director William Martin-Hurst had bought from General Motors in America.

Curiously, the P7 project was directly responsible for the naming of the P6 as the Rover 2000. Solihull's Sales Division had wanted to call it the 2-litre, but Martin-Hurst had pointed out to them that the P7 would then logically have to be called a 3-litre, and Rover already had a model by that name. So the name 2000 was chosen, much against the Sales Division's better judgment, with the name of 3000 in reserve for the P7 car.

Meanwhile, running more or less in parallel with the P7 and the five-cylinder projects had been a development programme on the four-cylinder engine. Jack Swaine's team found that by substituting bigger twin SU carburettors for the 2000's single SU, increasing the compression ratio to 10:1 and splitting the inlet manifold from the cylinder head (just as had been done for the IOE engines in 1962), they could get 124bhp out of the 1,978cc engine. A revised camshaft profile ensured that plenty of this new-found power was available at high rpm. As the five-cylinder 2½-litre was only putting out 125bhp or thereabouts, it was not surprising that the twin-carburettor engine was seized extras became options on the 2000TC.

The 2000TC was designed with the export market very firmly in view, so it was first seen in the European shop-window of the Geneva Motor Show in spring 1966. Home market models, which lacked some of the cosmetic innovations found on export cars, appeared that autumn. They were enthusiastically received; the TC offered vastly improved performance, with a top speed approaching 110mph and acceleration which put it into the sports car

In TC form, with twin SUs, the 1,978cc OHC engine gave 124bhp. Twin Weber 40 DCOEs had been tried during development, but they made the engine too intractable. In the search for more power, Rover had even fitted one development car with a Shorrocks supercharger, while Derrington offered a bolt-on twin-choke Weber conversion for the SC, which allegedly gave that car better performance than the production TC.

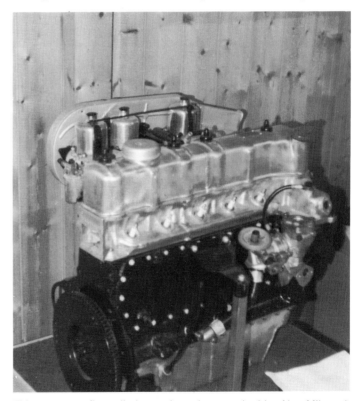

This prototype five-cylinder engine, photographed by Alan Milstead, is now preserved by BL Heritage. Weld seams on sump, cylinder head, rocker cover and air cleaner show that standard engines were 'cut and shut' to build the prototypes.

upon with enthusiasm by Rover's management and put into production as soon as it had proved itself (and gathered some advance publicity) in the works rally cars during 1964-65. Original plans were to introduce a plain 2000TC which would simply add the new engine to the base-model's specification, and a more sporting 2000S which would have the TC engine, wire wheels and various minor cosmetic alterations. In the end, the 2000S never got as far as the showrooms, although 15 cars were built, and its sporting

Before the crunch. The 3500 V8 engine installed in a P6 which is about to be subjected to the mandatory crash test at MIRA in 1970.

One that got away. A fuel-injected version of the V8 engine was planned for 1971 introduction, and the car (with manual transmission) would have been badged as a 3500EI, presumably standing for Electronic Injection, as the set of badges shows.

class. Without a doubt, it lost something in refinement as compared to the base model, and its fuel consumption was not as good, but it did provide an attractive alternative to the poorly-constructed European slingshots which were the only real performance saloons available at the time in the same price bracket. Most important of all to Rover was the American market, where the TC's reception by the motoring press was ecstatic; unfortunately, its relatively high purchase price seems to have deterred that nation's buyers, and the car ultimately failed to achieve what Rover had hoped for it there, despite heavy promotion of its safety features as well as its performance.

Introduced at the same time as the TC was the 2000

These two pictures show how the early production 2000s looked. Cars made between 1963 and 1966 had a single central reversing lamp, with reflectors incorporated in the tail-lamp clusters. Prior to 1968, the wheel covers had only a single decorative ring.

A longer nose was needed for the P7 six-cylinder cars. The first car, 17 EXK, was cobbled together, but by the time of the fourth prototype in 1964 (there were five altogether) Rover's stylists had come up with an attractive new front end.

Automatic. There were those at Solihull who thought it should never have been made, because it was far slower than the standard 2000, and the last thing the P6 needed was less performance. Nevertheless, Rover's Sales Division insisted that there was an 'old gentleman's' market for such a car, and this time they were proved right. Development began in about 1964, and the car was rushed through to production. It shared its Borg-Warner type 35 transmission with the Mk III 3-litre introduced in 1965, and used the same final drive as the standard 2000. As contemporary road tests noted, it lacked urge for acceleration because the torque band of the 2000 engine was really too narrow to suit an automatic transmission; it had to rev harder than the manual gearbox car to achieve the same speeds and so was noisier; and it used more petrol in return for less performance. That so many customers bought it is probably an indication of how

much the old sedate Rover image still overshadowed the radically different P6 in the mid-1960s!

Development of the base-model had, of course, never abated, and literally hundreds of minor improvements were introduced in the two-and-a-half years before the arrival of the TC and Automatic models. Among the most important were a new steering damper, which arrived in 1964, rear suspension changes in 1965, and a more powerful brake servo allied to new pad material in mid-1965. The cable-drive windscreen wipers were replaced by link-driven wipers, and there were also improvements to the cooling system.

The base model was redesignated 2000SC when the TC and Automatic models arrived, although it was never rebadged. While the very first TC models shared the positive-earth electrical system of the 2000, all three models

47 GYK was sold to Ted Eves of *Autocar,* and is now owned by a Rover enthusiast. Despite later claims that P7s were not as quick as the V8-engined P6Bs, the Experimental Department saw a genuine 140mph from this car – and the heavy nose even improved its handling!

changed to negative earth for the 1966 season to permit the use of standard transistorized electrical components. From about May 1966, Girling brakes replaced the original Dunlops; Girling had actually absorbed the Dunlop braking interests, but the new brakes also represented a distinct improvement, being both easier to service and less prone to the sticking pistons which in extreme cases could cause broken discs in the Dunlop installation. Nevertheless, early Girling-equipped cars had to be recalled when a brake pipe was found to chafe on the differential extension tube. Then, in the autumn of 1966, SC and Automatic models were given a new twin-silencer exhaust system. All three 2000 models gained a crossflow radiator in place of the vertical-flow type in 1968, and there was a repositioned carburettor air intake on the SC models, designed to avoid carburettor icing problems by picking up warm air from behind the radiator. The transmission oil cooler incorporated in the radiator on early TCs was now deleted, although it remained available as an option.

That 2000 developments were less numerous in the 1966-68 period is doubtless a reflection of the Company's preoccupation with work on the ex-Buick V8 engine. The story of how this 3½-litre power unit came to Rover has already been told (see Chapter 5), but it is interesting that when it first arrived at Solihull, Chief Engineer Peter Wilks failed to share his Managing Director's enthusiasm for it, pleading pressure of work from other projects. Not to be thwarted, William Martin-Hurst prevailed upon the Competitions Department, who had little to do because of a lull between rallies, to cut about a 2000 development car and bolt the Buick engine into it. He then took Spencer Wilks for a rapid motorway run in the car. Wilks senior was convinced at once, with the result that the V8 became a Rover engine in short order. Although the P5 was actually first into production with the new engine, most of the development work was carried out with P6 cars right from

The sporting image of the 2000TC was much enhanced by its optional wire wheels, which nevertheless remained rare and ceased to be available in late 1969. Without them, the TC could only be distinguished from the other 2000s by its badging.

the beginning.

Martin-Hurst had been quite right in his assessment that the V8 would fit into the P6 engine bay, but the adaptation was far from straightforward. A second development car was rebuilt around a Buick engine, with a minimum of panel alteration, but the cost penalty of production in this form would have been unacceptably high. In the end, Rover's engineers moved the front crossmember of the base-unit forwards, put the battery in the boot and canted the engine backwards slightly to get what they wanted – no increase in overall length, no undue front axle weight and no need for new bonnet or front wing panels. With detail alterations to the inner wings, and bonnet stiffeners modified to clear the repositioned crossmember, the V8 installation was complete.

Like the P7 engine before it, the V8 produced too much torque for the standard 2000 gearbox, so five of the six development cars were fitted with ZF five-speed gearboxes (the sixth had automatic transmission). Rover felt the ZF boxes were too unrefined, and after the 1967 Leyland takeover, they tried a Triumph 2000 gearbox in desperation. That was not the answer, either, and as there was no time to develop a new manual gearbox, the P6B (B for Buick again) went into production with a Borg-Warner type 35 automatic

transmission as the only available option. A stronger final drive casing was fitted to cope with the V8's torque and a higher 3.08:1 ratio aided fuel consumption and ensured a greater top speed than the four-cylinder cars; acceleration was no problem, even with the automatic gearbox! The V8-engined cars also had larger radiators, modified rear suspension mountings, increased spring rates and stronger dampers. Braking was improved by larger front discs and a bigger servo, while fatter tyres on wider offset wheels necessitated small changes in the front hubs in order to maintain the original track and turning circle.

The 3500, or Three Thousand Five as it was renamed at the last minute, was launched in April 1968 to an enthusiastic reception, although more than one commentator lamented the absence of a manual gearbox option. As usual, Rover were to be disappointed over export sales, but there were still high hopes of cracking the North American market, and for this purpose a special version of the P6B was introduced for the 1970 season. Not much needs to be said about the mechanical side of the 3500S, except that its exhaust emission-control equipment, Adwest Varamatic power-assisted steering and optional air conditioning all took engine power away from the back wheels, where it was

74

needed most. It could still outrun a 2000TC, but only just, and of course its fuel consumption had suffered. Dual-circuit braking looked good on the specification, and was never found on a home market P6, but the North American 3500S was a sales disaster. Only just over 2,000 were built, and the last of these were shipped hurriedly back to continental Europe for sale through Rover's dealer network there when the model was withdrawn in 1971. The stock of engines fitted with exhaust emission control was used up in the 1971 season home market 3500 cars with air conditioning.

The home market 3500 continued without significant mechanical change until the Mk II models arrived in the autumn of 1970. For 2000 models, the change to Mk II was marked by the introduction of an alternator in place of the dynamo, and by carburettor changes which had been brought about in the wake of emission-control development work. Base-unit commonization was served by putting the battery into the boot, 3500-fashion. The power-assisted steering first seen on the North American 3500S now became an option on the 3500, and the air conditioning system could also be specified at extra cost, although in practice it rarely was. The 2000TC models were given a distributor rev-limiter early in the 1971 season, governing engine speed to a 6,500rpm maximum. It seems that some owners had ignored the tachometer redline, probably in an attempt to out-accelerate hard-driven 3500s!

Much more interesting, however, was the October 1971 introduction of the long-awaited manual-transmission V8 model, which confusingly inherited the 3500S designation. The new gearbox in this car was simply an uprated 2000 four-speeder, with a strengthened and finned case, a much greater oil capacity and an oil pump driven from the rear of the layshaft. The gears themselves were shot-peened, and there were tougher layshaft bearings. Although the new clutch was criticized for being on the heavy side, no-one criticized the effect of the new transmission. The 3500S could cover the 0-60mph dash in a fraction over 9 seconds, gave vigorous acceleration right across its speed range, and peaked at 120mph or more – yet it still returned 25mpg. It had particular appeal as a Police chase car, as it undercut the price of the similarly rapid Jaguars by a huge margin, and

First thoughts on a facelift for the V8-engined cars included this late 1965 design with very Vauxhall-like styling details....

offered cheaper running costs as well. For the family motorist or executive it offered all the refinements and advantages of the 3500 (although certain cosmetic items standard on that car were extra-cost options on the 3500S), while giving him the opportunity to let his hair down with a real road-burner of a car at weekends. Not surprisingly, it was a big sales success.

Several changes to existing models coincided with the launch of the 3500S. The old four-fuse electrical system was replaced by the 12 fuse system of the North American 3500S. Manual transmission cars now had the gear lever attached directly to a gearbox extension, and there were internal changes to the 2000's manual gearbox. The 2000 models also received a pre-engaged starter, while the V8s were fitted with HIF type carburettors. All engines were now numbered in a Mk II series (1971 season Mk II cars

....but this was what went into production. This Three Thousand Five sports the revised wheel trims introduced in 1968 for all models, although the very first V8 cars had trims with the single central ring and improved claw fixings.

having in all cases Mk I engines). Subsequently, the V8 models were given a new alternator and starter motor, while the 2000 models were treated to yet another variety of exhaust system, this time with three silencer boxes, in an attempt to cut down the resonance which had plagued the four-cylinder cars ever since their introduction.

If the 3500S took the P6 into the high-performance class where it had really belonged from the beginning the four-cylinder models were beginning to look decidedly slow by the early 1970s. If road-test figures are to be trusted, the changes over the years had actually impaired their performance by comparison with early models, and to some extent the Rover 2000 had assumed the mantle of the earlier P4s and P5s – a good, sensible car without much performance. The problem was compounded because the cheap end of the

executive market at which the 2000 had originally been pitched was demanding – and getting – more and more performance. Rover therefore started to look around for ways of giving the four-cylinder models more punch.

For a time, Solihull considered giving the P6 a new four-cylinder 2,205cc DOHC engine, which was also intended in the longer term for use in the cheaper versions of the P10. Early in 1971, the P10 became a joint Rover-Triumph project (see Chapter 7), and a six-cylinder Triumph engine was planned for the cheaper models. As the DOHC engine now had no long-term future its development was aborted. Designed by David Wall to be machined on existing P6 transfer line tooling, it had a projected power output of between 120 and 145bhp (although fuel-injected prototypes gave 170bhp) and would have been installed with

Export models often differed in detail from their home market equivalents, and this attractive beast is a Three Thousand Five to German specification. The Rostyle wheels, thin side trim strips and racing mirror were available in the UK, but the problem was finding a dealer who knew that!

a slant of 35 degrees to ensure underbonnet clearance. One prototype of the engine, which was the last all-new, all-Rover, power unit ever designed, is preserved by BL Heritage.

With the slant-four option gone, Rover turned to an over-bored 2000 unit, also of 2,205cc capacity, for the revamped 'small' P6. New carburettors anticipated European emission-control regulations, and effectively prevented the full performance potential from being realized, but the larger engine's wider torque band gave the autumn 1973 2200 models (SC, TC and SC Automatic) a flexibility and mid-range urge which had been absent from the smaller 'fours'; the Automatic particularly benefited. Unfortunately fuel consumption was worse on all versions, although this seemed to matter little in the days before the Yom Kippur War when the 2200 was being developed, and there was some compensation in the engine's greater refinement. There were also improved ignition suppression and engine warm-up on the TC, the latter achieved by a thermostatically-controlled engine air intake.

Parts standardization and the increase in engine torque meant that the 2200 models inherited the stronger differential design and rear suspension of the 3500 variants. Although 2200SC Automatics retained the 2000's Borg-

Warner type 35 gearbox, the 3500 models had a new type 65 gearbox; lighter than the type 35, it offered smoother changes and was said to be more durable. The same year, the 3500 and 3500S became the first cars in the world to be offered with Dunlop Denovo run-flat tyres as an extra-cost option, available only with PAS. Early examples of these tyres gained a reputation for rapid wear, however, and relatively few P6Bs were so equipped. Meanwhile, 1974 season V8 engines had new pistons to give a lower compression ratio suitable for four-star (97 octane) fuel, although the consequent power and acceleration losses were never acknowledged in Rover literature. To some extent, the power loss (around 7bhp overall) was offset on the automatics because they now had the bigger-bore exhaust system of the 'S', which restored about 6bhp and gave the two models identical power outputs. Mechanical specification of all models thereafter remained without significant change until P6 production ceased in 1976, the V8 models ceding to the new SD1 3500 in the summer of that year and the 2200s continuing until Christmas, when the P6 lines were finally closed down. The very last car – a left-hand-drive 2200TC – was inexplicably sold off, but BL Heritage were able to preserve the last of the V8-engined cars. The 2200 models remained catalogued until the summer of 1977,

Another export car – this time a North American 3500S. Note the air scoops, fatter front bumper, bolt-through wheel trims, Icelert sensor and additional lights. The thicker side trim strips were later standardized on Mk II cars, and the blacked-out horizontal surfaces of the grille were inspired by Zagato's TCZ prototype.

but thereafter were replaced by the SD1 2300 model.

Although the 3,528cc V8 was the largest engine offered in production cars, British Leyland did build two 4½-litre cars for racing (see Chapter 7), and eight 4500 models are said to have been assembled in Australia, using the 4,416cc long-stroke version of the V8 originally developed for the P8 saloon, but only put into production in Australia in 1973 for Leyland Australia's products. In standard form, as fitted to the Leyland P76 car, this engine developed 192bhp at 4,250rpm and 285lb/ft of torque at 2,500rpm (SAE gross figures), although some production versions were made in a higher state of tune. The Rover 4500s were allegedly capable of 130mph.

**Body and interior**

From beginning to end of its 13½-year production run, the P6 used basically the same bodyshell. In the early days of the car's conception, David Bache – designing this time in his own right – had reasoned that the base-unit construction with bolt-on panels would make subsequent facelifts via restyled panels both cheap and easy, but no such facelift ever came about, and an early plan for a two-door Sports model never progressed beyond the mock-up stage. The only styling changes introduced were cosmetic, which perhaps suggests as much as anything that Bache got the shape right first time and that there was never any need for new panel designs!

Before production commenced, however, Bache had a hard time 'getting it right'. His first thoughts for the P6 were strongly reminiscent of Virgil Exner's 1956 Chrysler Dart prototype (rather than of Citroen's DS, as is commonly supposed). At the time, Bache was keen on American styling, and his first quarter-scale clays featured tailfins as well as the sloping nose shared by the Dart and the DS. Maurice Wilks and Robert Boyle soon talked him out of the tailfins, but the sloping nose was still in evidence by the time of the first P6 prototype in February 1959. Spencer and Maurice Wilks were not happy, however, and the collective foot of management was put firmly down the following year. All subsequent prototypes (about six had already been built)

This Mk II 2000 displays a number of optional extras including front seat head restraints, overriders and the boot lid mounting for the spare wheel (covered by a decorative disc bearing the Rover emblem). The reversing lights had been incorporated in the lamp clusters since 1966, while the reflectors had moved from boot lid to wings in 1971. Badging apart, 2200 models would be visually identical.

had the familiar production nose design, which cost the car some 5mph in top speed through its inferior aerodynamics. Typically for the early 1960s, the new nose featured an American-inspired twin headlamp arrangement.

The P6 body could not have been more unlike its predecessors. Lower and less fussy-looking, it retained an air of dignity which gave it credible links with Rover's past, but the patrician image of the P4s and P5s had gone. Trim-strips were out, and badging was kept to a minimum in the best Rover tradition. Bache relied on simple styling with just a body swage-line to bring down the high waistline characteristic of all his Rover designs (both the P5 and the SD1 have it too). The whole design had a classical elegance and a timelessness which even transcended the arrival of curved side window glass in the early 1960s, a styling catalyst which gave designers greater freedom in the shapes of their

passenger cabins. In prototype form, the petrol tank was installed under the boot floor, but this overstressed the rear of the base-unit, and so the tank was resited above the back axle. William Martin-Hurst worried that the boot was now too small, so he persuaded Maurice Wilks to engineer a large recess into the boot floor (after the body tools had been made!) and to make available an optional external mounting for the spare wheel on the boot lid so that more space was freed for luggage.

Changes to the appearance of the standard home market 2000 were minimal before the introduction of Mk II models in 1970. A locking petrol cap was standardized during 1965 and a new front lower valance was fitted the following year, which gave better airflow to the radiator and allegedly increased the top speed by about 1mph. The 1966 season cars had twin reversing lamps incorporated in the tail-light

The quickest production P6 of all, a manual-transmission 3500S. Like all Mk II models, this car has the new bonnet panel and grille, new door handles, plate-type badges and side trim strips. Blacked-out sills and vinyl-covered rear quarter-panels were also Mk II features, but the vinyl roof was peculiar to the 3500S at first. The early 3500S cars had the bolt-through wheel trims seen in this picture.

clusters instead of the single central lamp of the first cars, and the reflectors displaced by this change were resited on the bottom corners of the boot lid. The 1969 models all had new hubcaps with improved claw fixings (the earlier ones tended to rotate and could even cut through tyre valves), which were identified by two black rings in the centre. During that season, a new through-flow ventilation system was introduced, with flap valves concealed within the rear quarter-pillars. The opening rear quarter-lights were now redundant and were replaced by fixed panes, but within a year the original system had been reinstated. All the four-cylinder Mk I cars had chromed 2000 badges on the boot lid and front wings, plus TC badges in both these places and on the bonnet when appropriate. Automatics were so identified by an additional badge on the boot lid and a few early cars also had this badge on the front wings. Some of the very last Mk I cars actually had the badging associated with Mk IIs, probably because stocks of the earlier badges ran out before the planned changeover.

Options, of course, were legion, although many of them

remained rare because they were little publicized. One which was frequently seen was the Webasto fabric sunroof, which was an approved post-factory extra from the beginning; almost never seen, however, were the two types of sliding steel sunroof offered after autumn 1968 (by Coenan and Hollandia) and the glass roof panel, produced by Triplex in conjunction with Rover, and available from 1969 as a post-factory fitting by Roof Installations Ltd. It had a zip-in headlining, so that the car could be used as a normal closed saloon, or as a splendidly light and airy vehicle without the disadvantages of a convertible top.

It was possible to have as options on the home market 2000s many of the features which were standard on Export models. Thus, from 1966, a thin stainless steel trim strip could be added along the body swage-line, chromed Rostyle wheels were available and rubber-faced overriders of a pleasant squat design could be specified. The Icelert system, a temperature sensor fitted ahead of the grille which lit a dashboard light to warn of the possibility of ice on the roads, was also available. In practice, though, these options

The neat and impressive dashboard layout of a 1967 2000TC.

The P6's main fault was a lack of interior space, particularly in the rear. These are the box-pleated Ambla seats standard on the original 3500S; on other models, leather seat facings were standard until 1973, when nylon cloth took over.

This revised instrument panel was first seen on the North American 3500S, and was standardized on Mk II V8 and 2000TC models.

were rarely taken up by home market customers. Equally rare were the wire wheels available on TC models, and an alternative design of rubber-faced overrider which was introduced in 1965 but remained unpopular because it did not suit the P6 shape at all. North American customers could specify a second type of Rostyle wheel, a rather vulgar creation known as the MagStar, but this was never available in the UK. A heated rear window was a popular option from the beginning, as were front fog lights slung under the bumper, but Sundym tinted glass and Delaney Gallay air conditioning, both introduced in August 1969, were rarely seen on home market cars.

Body differences for the Three Thousand Five were kept to a minimum, but the cars were instantly recognizable by a heavy stainless steel 'eyebrow' at the leading edge of the bonnet and a deeper front valance to accommodate the larger radiator. In addition, the squat rubber-faced overriders were standard, and there were 3500 plate-type badges (engraved rather than printed like the Mk II variety) on wings, grille and boot lid, plus 'V8' badges on the bonnet and boot lid.

Sharp eyes might also have spotted a new lashing ring at the front of the base-unit and a thinner surround to the triangular grille badge than on the 2000.

The first indications of Rover's thinking about the forthcoming Mk II models were given by the North American 3500S cars when they appeared for the 1970 season. These had new bolt-through wheel trims of a sporty 'spoked' design, and side trim strips which were noticeably wider than the early optional or Export type; twin door mirrors were also fitted. The Icelert system was standard, and the cars were also distinguished by a number of features which would never be available for the home market. Thus, there were a fatter front bumper and three air intake scoops on the bonnet to aid engine bay cooling, while the horizontal surfaces of the grille were blacked-out (an idea derived from the 1965 Zagato coupe prototype). A painted coachline was also added above the side trim strip, and the cars had the special side lights and marker lights demanded by US Federal Regulations. These same regulations obliged Rover to incorporate crash-reinforcement bars inside the doors.

The prototype 2000 two-door drop-head by FLM Panelcraft was commissioned by Rover in 1965. It is currently owned by the author. The roof panel of Triplex Sundym glass fitted to the 2000TC was designed to demonstrate how glass could be used in vehicle construction as an alternative to metal.

Although the 3500S Automatics were allegedly produced in both Mk I and Mk II forms, they were always curious hybrids, and in fact some of the Mk I cars sold off in Europe were updated by dealers with Mk II grilles.

All the Mk II P6s used the 3500 base-unit with its revised front crossmember and the battery box in the boot. Known in sales literature as 'New Look' models, they were distinguished by a black plastic radiator grille, the thick side trim strips of the 3500S Automatics, new hubcaps with a black centre panel, and a bonnet with two 'power bulges', which in fact acted as stiffeners and replaced the cross-bracing found inside earlier bonnets. All Mk IIs had black or (less commonly) brown vinyl panels on the rear quarter-pillars, with a P5 Coupe-style Viking ship badge, and from autumn 1971 customers could specify as an option on the 3500 the matching vinyl roof covering which was standard on the new 3500S. In all cases, the body sills were painted to match the vinyl panels in an attempt to slim the car's side elevation. The TC models had rubber-faced overriders like the V8s, and the few 1971 season cars

The 2200SC, introduced in 1973 and featuring an over-bored version of the 2000 engine, brought a welcome improvement in torque, but a less pleasing increase in fuel consumption.

KXC 202M

(mainly 3500s) fitted with air conditioning had a single air scoop on the bonnet, though later air conditioned cars dispensed with this. New door handles on the Mk IIs looked neater than the early type, and the rear reflectors were repositioned below the light clusters as part of a series of rear-end changes. The marque name moved from the centre of the boot lid to its bottom left-hand corner, while other changes were to the '2000' badge (which was now in aluminium with a black background) and to the position of the triangular grille badge (resited on the bonnet). The 'V8' and 'TC' badges moved from bonnet to grille, and the 3500 – the Three Thousand Five name chosen by William Martin-Hurst was now dropped – lost its 'eyebrow'. Further badging alterations accompanied the launch of the manual-transmission 3500S in autumn 1971; plate-type badges replaced the 2000's model badge, matching badges on all cars bore the 'Rover' name on the boot lid, and Borg-Warner-equipped 2000s lost their 'Automatic' badge.

The 3500S models inherited the bolt-through wheel trims of their North American namesakes (and supplies were also used up on certain other Export vehicles), but were fitted with the standard trims after autumn 1973. On this date, which coincided with the launch of the 2200 models, all cars were fitted with a driver's door mirror as standard to conform to new EEC Regulations. The heated rear window was now standard in all but certain Export markets, and Sundym glass was standardized on V8-engined models. All the P6 cars built from early 1976 were sprayed in the new paint plant built for the SD1 at Solihull, using SD1 colours and the new 'oven-bake' paint process. In order to facilitate this, body panels met their base-units earlier in the assembly process than had hitherto been the case. Sadly, the new paint process had teething troubles, and Rover were plagued with warranty claims on these last P6s (as on early SD1s) when the paint started to flake. A batch of 150 of the last 3500 models was built as a 'limited edition', and these cars were known in the trade as 'VIP' models. All were finished in Platinum, the silver metallic paint used on SD1s, but not otherwise available on the P6.

The story of the P6's interior development is no less

84

complicated than that of its exterior appearance. When it was launched in 1963, its leather-covered seats were of completely new design, light in weight and carefully padded for optimum body support, and the rear seat was designed strictly to seat two. Some contemporary road tests described these seats as the most comfortable available in any car, bar none. Weight and cost had also been saved by the use of Formica imitation wood on plastic strips for the door cappings and on the dashboard (although a batch of early cars did have real wood veneer trim). The dashboard itself was an entirely new design by David Bache's team, with a full-width parcel shelf running just below the windscreen and glove boxes repositioned at knee height, with drop-down lids made of plastic which would crush in an accident. The whole dashboard was a single lightweight plastic moulding, grained to look like leather – Bache has said that to get the desired effect he made a dashboard, covered it in leather and had the moulds taken directly from it! Instruments, in typical Bache style, were in a separate 'pod' superimposed on the parcel shelf and consisted of a fashionable strip-type

Zagato's Lancia-like styling exercise on a 2000S – the TCZ. Changes of registration number have fuelled unfounded rumours that more than one car was built. The TCZ has been restored by an enthusiast, and is seen here at a club rally in 1982, when it was photgraphed by Lesley Ann Taylor.

David Bache's two-door hatchback coupe based on a Three Thousand Five was built for Rover by Harold Radford in 1967. It has always been known at Rover as 'Gladys'. The nose recalls P7 designs, the bonnet bulges appeared on Mk II P6s, and the box-pleated seats are pure 3500S. Bache now owns this car, which allegedly cost £22,000 to build.

speedometer, plus petrol and water temperature gauges, with all other functions reduced to warning lights in a row across the top. Switchgear was carefully laid out along the edge of the parcel shelf, with switches of different shapes to aid identification. A central console carried trinket trays and provision for a radio, while the handbrake moved back to its pre-P4 position on the transmission tunnel.

The first interior change was the addition of a steady prop to the rear view mirror in late 1964. Later in the 1965 model-year, the mirror support was fitted with a courtesy light to replace the rather temperamental lights fitted at the dashboard ends on early cars. This courtesy light in turn disappeared along with the interior light over the rear window when a centrally-mounted roof lamp arrived with the Three Thousand Five models in 1968, although the rear-mounted light was retained when a sunroof was fitted.

Front and rear headrests could be supplied from 1965, those on the front requiring a revised seat back with internal mounting brackets, which was later standardized, and bar-type front seat adjusters replaced the cable-operated type towards the end of 1967. Meanwhile, a 120mph speedometer had replaced the 115mph original with the introduction of the TC cars in 1966, and there had been new knobs for the heater, choke and petrol reserve controls. The TC itself had a rev-counter and a resited clock, and this facia change became optional for other models. Early TCs had a 'TC' badge on the radio speaker panel and a further TC-related option was an imitation-wood-rimmed steering wheel with a matching wooden gear lever knob.

The only interior changes made for the Three Thousand Five were a 140mph speedometer with a black instead of chromed bezel, a 'V8' badge on the radio speaker panel and a '3500' badge on the steering wheel, but major changes came with the North American 3500S. Some of these were later standardized on Mk II models, like the instrument layout with four round dials instead of a rectangular box, new internally-illuminated switchgear, non-adjustable front seat head restraints, bigger front door armrests and turnwheel-operated front quarter-lights. The standard seats anticipated the manual transmission 3500S by being covered in the perforated vinyl known as Ambla, and having

box-pleating which David Bache has said was originally designed for the aborted P8 saloon. Leather was an option not often specified, although all the cars did have a leather-covered steering wheel rim. Air conditioning, which brought with it Sundym glass, was a commonly-specified option. Many 3500S items would never reach the home market cars, however. Thus the boot area was far more comprehensively carpeted than that of the Mk II models (the Denovo-shod cars excepted), and there were electric window lifts, a colour-keyed console panel and handbrake gaiter, and rigid map pockets beneath the front door armrests. The Mk II models' interiors varied rather more than the Mk Is'. Even though all of them had the new front armrests, turnwheel-operated quarter-lights, and darker 'wood' trim, only the 2000TC and V8-engined cars had the new switchgear and the new instrument panel with its round dials. Box-pleated Ambla upholstery was an uncommon 2000SC-only option, and brushed nylon seat facings could be had in Sandalwood (Ebony soon became available, and Bronze replaced Sandalwood for 1973). Ambla upholstery was standardized on the manual-transmission 3500S in order to keep this model's base-price below that of its automatic equivalent, although leather remained available as an extra-cost option.

The next round of revisions coincided with the introduction of the 2200 models for the 1974 season. All three manual-gearbox cars had a longer gear lever, while non-adjustable front seat head restraints were standardized on both V8-engined models; first seen on the North American 3500S, these were optionally available on 2200s. All models lost the parking lights switch, and the 3500S lost its Ambla upholstery. All across the range, seats were henceforth to a box-pleated pattern, and leather was relegated to an option in place of the standard corded brushed-nylon coverings. Front seats also had modified backrests to give more legroom in the rear (and, unintentionally, less comfort in the front), while there was a new convex rear-view mirror on a collapsible safety stem, with reshaped sun visors to fit round it. Shortly after the 2200's introduction, a cheaper tufted carpet material available in brown only was used on all models, but the only subsequent

Graber made two coupes out of left-hand-drive P6s. This is his 1967 design on a 2000TC; the later show car was generally similar, but was based on a Three Thousand Five.

changes were made for the limited-edition 3500 'VIP' models, which had SD1-type seat fabric and headlining and 3500S Automatic-type air conditioning as standard.

Special-bodied P6s were, of course, limited in number because of the relative inflexibility of the base-unit structure. The earliest conversion was carried out in 1965 by FLM Panelcraft on Peter Wilks' instructions. This was a two-door convertible based on a standard 2000 and had actually been inspired by Panelcraft's 1964 P5 convertible for a private customer which Wilks had inspected. Panelcraft also built an estate prototype from a 2000 in 1966. Meanwhile, Rover commissioned the Italian coachbuilder Zagato to build a two-door fastback coupe from a 1965 2000S (twin-carburettor), and David Bache designed his own two-door fastback on a 3500 base-unit in 1966-67, which would probably have worn the badge of Rover's Alvis subsidiary if it had ever gone into production. The mid-1960s also saw at least three 'specials' built by the Swiss coachbuilder Graber. These included a 2000 two-door convertible in 1966, a 2000TC two-door coupe the following year, and a 3500 two-door coupe in 1968.

It was principally the British Leyland takeover in 1967 which killed off production prospects for the Rover-commissioned 'specials', but the estate car variant *was* built in limited numbers, albeit as an aftermarket conversion by FLM Panelcraft, not a production model by Rover. Briefly known as the Panelcraft Estoura, the car was at first marketed exclusively by Crayford Auto Development (and these cars bear a Crayford badge), then by Hurst Park Automobiles of East Molesey, Surrey, and after 1970 by H.R. Owen, when it became known rather misleadingly as the 'Owen conversion'. Conversions were available on used as well as new cars and after 1968, a 3500 version could be obtained. The 2000 and 2000TC estates remained rare because they were too expensive for a market already well covered by Triumph's 2000 estate. The 3500 estate was a success, however, and before production stopped in 1976, a few 3500S estates with manual transmission had been built.

Exact figures are not available, but it seems that between 150 and 160 P6 estates were built. There were some minor

FLM Panelcraft's estate conversion on P6 models offered 49.5 cubic feet of load space.

variations over the years, the most significant being the addition on H.R. Owen cars of an electric fuel pump in place of the mechanical one to overcome airlock problems with the special fuel tanks fitted to the estates. Even though load-carrying space in the cars was limited by a sloping roofline, which also hindered rearward visibility, the 3500 versions sold tolerably well for a few years to the sort of customer who was prepared to pay just a little extra to get something out of the ordinary.

If the professional classes who had always formed the core of Rover's clientele accepted the P6 as a quality car in the Rover tradition, they were not fooled into thinking it shared the exclusivity of its forebears – the sheer numbers in which it was produced saw to that. Although Solihull had allowed plant capacity initially for 500 cars a week (maximum production volume of the P4 had been around 280 cars a week in the 1954 model year), it rapidly became clear that this was not enough. A series of industrial disputes in the mid-1960s ensured a permanent waiting list for the standard car, and this must have discouraged attempts to put rebodied versions into production. In the middle of 1972, Solihull was finally able to increase production targets to 1,000 cars per week; by this stage, customers were having to wait four to six months for a 3500S, although delivery times for the 2000 models were rather shorter. Over 329,000 P6s were built – the exact total is in dispute – huge volumes by Rover standards, but tiny compared to British Leyland's rosy vision of production figures for the P6's successor, the SD1.

# CHAPTER 6

# Rover's swansong

## The SD1, 1976–1986

**SD1 3500 (1976-1980), V8-S (1979-1980), 3500SE (1980-1986), 3500 Vanden Plas (1980-1986), Vitesse (1982-1986), and Vanden Plas EFi (1984-1986); 2600 (1977-1980), 2600S (1980-1986), 2600SE (1982-1984) and 2600 Vanden Plas (1984-1986); 2300 (1977-1986) and 2300S (1980-1986); 2400SD Turbo (1982-1985); 2000 (1982-1986)**

By the time of the next new Rover saloon, the old Rover Company had changed beyond all recognition. Indeed, what had once been Rover no longer actually existed, but had become part of the Specialist Division of British Leyland which was responsible for sports cars, luxury saloons and Land-Rovers. From that name of Specialist Division came the codename of SD1 under which the new car was developed, the '1' denoting that it was the division's first project.

After the merger which created British Leyland in 1968, Rover initially retained its autonomy to a large extent, but by the early 1970s BL had started the difficult process of rationalizing the various marques it now owned. It was obvious that the company needed only one range of saloons to replace the directly competitive Triumph 2000/2500 and Rover P6 2000/3500 models. During 1971, the Rover and Triumph design engineers both put in bids to develop that new range of saloons, and Rover's P10 proposal was chosen over Triumph's Puma. The project was rechristened RT 1 ('Rover-Triumph, no.1') when the engineering departments of the two companies were merged shortly afterwards, and

soon after that it was again renamed as SD1 when Rover-Triumph became the Specialist Division.

SD1 was therefore a Rover from the beginning, and it was Rover engineers who took the lead in its design and development. Rover's Spen King was by this stage in overall control of Rover-Triumph engineering (having spent a period as Triumph's Chief Engineer immediately after the BL merger); Rover's David Bache was in charge of styling; and Rover's Gordon Bashford was responsible for the overall layout and 'chassis' design. There was also continuity of engineering in that the flagship variants of SD1 were planned to have the Rover V8 engine. Nevertheless, for the cheaper versions of the car, BL decided to use a new six-cylinder engine which was already under development by Triumph. The rest of the drivetrain was to be shared between the SD1 and the forthcoming Triumph TR7 and TR8 sports cars. Thus the rear axle and both the manual and automatic gearboxes were designed to suit both applications.

All this was obviously carefully planned to minimize capital expenditure on production tooling, and the ruthless cost-paring which BL's planners and accountants indulged in at this period resulted in the SD1 being built down to a price. No previous Rover had ever been conceived in such a way, and the inevitable compromises caused some equally inevitable dissatisfaction among existing Rover customers who loyally bought the new car. Despite ecstatic initial reactions from the press, and the award of European Car of the Year for 1977 by an international jury, quality control

The original 3500 was an undeniably stylish car, and incorporated a lot of new technology. To combat the rust which had afflicted P5 and P6 Rovers, the sills were pressure-ventilated to prevent moisture build-up.

problems in the SD1's early days quickly earned the car a bad reputation. The collapse of large-car sales which followed the 1979 oil crisis then terminally damaged BL's hopes of selling the SD1 in anything like the quantities originally planned.

Although vastly improved build quality, a wider model range, and a successful racing programme pulled the car round during the early 1980s, total sales never remotely approached the combined totals of the Rover P6 and Triumph saloons which the SD1 had replaced – and in fact did not even equal the totals achieved by the P6 alone. The huge new plant which BL had built at Solihull for SD1 assembly never was used to the full for Rover saloons; from 1980, part of it was turned over to Triumph TR7 assembly; and then at the end of 1981 it was closed and the SD1 assembly lines were relocated in the old Morris plant at Cowley. By this stage, BL's Specialist Division had already fragmented, first into Jaguar-Rover-Triumph in the later 1970s and then even further after 1978 when Land Rover was established as a separate operating company. Rover, or what remained of it, joined the old Volume Cars division

and during 1982 the resulting BL business unit took on the name of Austin-Rover.

The SD1 was undoubtedly dogged by misfortune in its early life, and it never did get the better of its direct rival the Ford Granada, let alone compete effectively with the medium-sized Mercedes and BMW saloons which made such inroads into the British market in the early 1980s. Yet for all that, it was a car with considerable character. Its striking shape remained distinctive a decade after the last example had been built; the performance and refinement of the larger-engined models were excellent; and the later cars with the full Vanden Plas-specification wood and leather trim were certainly worthy heirs to the Rover name.

**Body and interior**
David Bache's proposal to make the new Rover a sleek five-door hatchback saloon was a radical one for the early 1970s, and was undoubtedly what persuaded BL management to choose the Rover design in preference to Triumph's conservative Puma. However, the development of Bache's styling proposal did not proceed smoothly.

Although the basic dimensions were all in place by the end of 1971, the full-size styling buck was angular and undistinguished.

Bache realized he had to do something radical – and he did just that. He borrowed a Maserati Ghibli from a friend, called in the styling staff over a weekend, and had them graft the Maserati's curves onto the full-size styling buck. With the addition of some stylish lamp units at the front which had clearly been inspired by the contemporary Ferrari Daytona, the SD1 was completely transformed, and by the Monday morning a stunning production style was ready for the enthusiastic approval of BL management.

Right from the beginning, BL's cost-conscious approach to the SD1 ensured that it would have a monocoque body shell: monocoques were much cheaper to build than exotic structures like the P6's base-unit with its bolt-on panels. In addition, the latest developments in structural engineering allowed the SD1 monocoque to be made strong enough to

Front aspect of an early SD1 3500 showing the skeletal version of the traditional Rover shield badge on the bonnet and the twin auxiliary lamps recessed beneath the bumper.

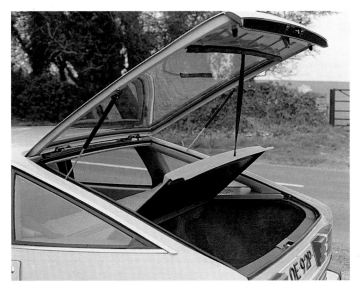

The SD1's wide-open rear hatch lifts the extended parcels tray which doubles as a security cover for the boot area.

give good refinement and meet the severest crash-safety requirements without incurring an unacceptable weight penalty. Even the windscreen – bonded to the shell rather than fitted in the conventional way – was made to contribute to the monocoque's torsional stiffness.

The SD1's production life can be divided into three distinct periods, and each one of those was marked by visual as well as engineering changes. The first period lasted from the car's launch in June 1976 until September 1980. The second period was really a transitional phase, and lasted from October 1980 until January 1982. The cars assembled at Cowley in the third and final period then had several very obvious differences from the earlier models. Production ran out in the first half of 1986, and the SD1 was replaced in the Rover range by the 800-series saloons, which Austin-Rover had developed jointly with the Japanese Honda company.

*The 1977-1980 models*

These first SD1s were characterized by stainless steel bumpers with black plastic end caps. Their headlamps were set back from the front panel, and the wraparound front lamp clusters incorporated both side lamps and indicators. The rear panel carried two silver plinth badges, printed in black with identifying details of the model. Wheels were steel discs with different trims according to model. The 3500s initially had stainless steel trims with black-painted sections; the 2600s had grey plastic trims of the same 'clover-leaf' design, also with black-painted sections; and the 2300s had all-grey trims. Attractive multi-spoked alloys

The plain wheel trims and, of course, the rear badge mark this car out as a 2300 model.

Showing the alloy wheels optional on other models is this V8-S, the luxury edition of the 3500. Note the black bumpers, the 'V8' wing badge and the coachline. By this stage, the original skeletal bonnet badge had been replaced by a more traditional type.

in a natural metal finish were extra-cost options on 3500 and 2600 models, and came with low-profile tyres. Denovo run-flat tyres were also available, on special steel wheels.

Metallic paint finishes were advertised from the beginning, but in practice they seem not to have been available until early 1978 or thereabouts. This was almost certainly because of teething troubles with the new paint plant at Solihull. In theory, the thermoplastic process of passing an electric charge through the bodyshell and charging the paint with the opposite polarity should have caused the paint to adhere smoothly and uniformly, but in practice water often became trapped under the paint, leading to blemishes and flaking. Early cars were available in an uninspiring selection of red, white, brown and yellow, and the addition of a rather lurid green in 1977 did nothing to improve the picture.

The rather drab selection of light and dark browns chosen for the interior trim was typical of the period, and the door trims were rather cheap-looking injection-moulded plastic items. All upholstery was in cloth – there was no leather option at first – and 3500s and 2600s shared the same box-pleated upholstery, while the base-model 2300 had more heavily pleated seat covers. An ingenious modular dashboard design (entry-level 2300s simply had the rev

Successor to the V8-S was the Vanden Plas. This 1981 car shows off the shaded alloy wheels, rubber bump-strips on the flanks and bumpers, the black badge plinths and the bright-finished tailpipe.

counter unit missing) simplified production by being readily adaptable for left-hand or right-hand steering. However, its build quality was often atrocious, its black finish uninspired, and the lack of lighting for the switchgear made night driving tiresome. Standard central locking and optional electric windows may have been welcome on the early 3500s, and the expensive Triplex Ten-Twenty windscreen (which combined the best features of zone-toughened and laminated glass for increased safety) may have looked good on the specification. However, none of these were enough to offset the SD1's other shortcomings. This was not what Rover customers expected – and they made their views clear by turning to rival marques.

Rover recognized fairly quickly that something had to be done. However, improvements and upgrades took their time to work through the system and not much changed before the 1980 model-year which started in October 1979. The first specification upgrades to the 3500 were made in October 1977, when the car was differentiated from the two new six-cylinder models by taking on a passenger door mirror, electric windows and a four-speaker radio-cassette system as standard; all these items had earlier been optional and now became options on the sixes. At the same time, the

single supporting strap of the rear parcels shelf was changed for two straps, and the chromed windscreen washer nozzles were replaced by domed plastic items.

Customer demand next forced Rover to make leather upholstery an option in April 1978, although it was available only in a single colour (Nutmeg brown) and had a disappointingly small take-up rate. For the 1979 season which began in October 1978, rear seat belts were standardized on the 3500, and then black paint was added to the options list in February 1979.

All this time, Rover had been working on a higher specification for the SD1's eventual launch onto the US market. The 1980 models which arrived in autumn 1979 would preview many of the changes made to suit transatlantic demands, but they themselves were previewed in June 1979 by the new V8-S model. This new top-of-the-range Rover was mechanically unchanged from the 3500, but came with several new features. Externally, it was distinguished by black bumpers, coachlines on the body sides and a bright exhaust tailpipe finisher. The unique rear badging was on black plinths, and the cars wore a traditional Rover Viking ship badge on their bonnets instead of the unloved skeletal one seen on the first cars. The first

The 2600, which offered 136bhp, proved to be a popular choice for SD1 buyers who wanted a more economical alternative to the 3500.

900 examples also had gold-finished alloy wheels, unless equipped with Denovos, although natural-finish alloys were supplied for cars painted in metallic silver. Many V8-S models came in Triton green metallic paint – another strangely lurid choice which looked better on the Triumph sports cars with which it was shared and was almost never ordered on any other SD1.

All V8-S models had the sliding sunroof, a tinted anti-glare band across the top of the windscreen, and a headlamp wash-wipe system. Inside, there were leather upholstery (although cross-ribbed velvet was optional), four head restraints with detachable cushions, and shag-pile carpets. The dashboard and console carried bright high-lights, and air conditioning was standard. With this came an additional cool air intake in the form of a slot in the car's front panel, between bonnet and bumper.

With the 1980 models which went on sale in November 1979, subtle upgrades accompanied the spread to other models of many V8-S features. The traditional Viking ship bonnet badge now replaced the skeletal type completely, and the rear plinth badges had larger lettering. Alloy wheels became standard on 3500 models, and an alloy Denovo wheel was introduced to suit these. The 2600s took on the 3500s' stainless steel trims, and the 2300s took on the 2600s' painted plastic ones; in each case, however, the centre badge changed from the skeletal Viking ship to a less schematic representation. Air conditioning and the headlamp wash-wipe system became optional (though both remained very rare), and the carpet inserts on the rear parcels shelf both improved its appearance and stopped items sliding about on its smooth injection-moulded plastic.

*The 1981 models*
With the 1981 cars introduced in October 1980, Rover finally got the SD1 fundamentally right – although quality control of electrical equipment in particular remained patchy. Body production had been transferred from Castle Bromwich to Cowley earlier in the year, and a revised paint process – with the polarity of the charges reversed from the earlier method – ensured that the paint not only went on thickly but also stayed where it was put. A range of bright and attractive new colours rejuvenated the cars' appearance, and these were matched by revitalized interiors.

The range had also been realigned. While a 2300 was still the entry model, there was a better-equipped 2300S above that. Next up came a 2600S; above that, the standard V8-engined car had become a 3500SE, and right at the top of the range stood the Vanden Plas – a name new to Rover. In earlier times, Vanden Plas had been a distinguished coachbuilder, but after the company's purchase by Austin in 1946, the name appeared on various up-market Austins until BL acquired it in the 1968 merger.

All models of SD1 now had the front air intake slot. In addition, they had bright metal door mirror housings – so much more attractive than the drab black rubber items of the earlier cars – and the two V8-powered models had twin coachlines and black rubber bump strips on their bumpers. The Vanden Plas came with headlamp washer jets in large rubber overriders, and these could be fitted at extra cost to other models. Other special features of the Vanden Plas exterior were black rear plinth badges, a bright tailpipe finisher, and grey-enamelled alloy wheels.

The front wings of the two V8 models now carried bright 'V8' badges, while those of the 2600 models carrried a '2600' badge. Tinted glass was standard on the V8s and optional on other models, but the expensive Ten-Twenty windscreen had gone – a casualty, no doubt, of increasing manufacturing costs associated with the generally higher specification levels. Nevertheless, the Vanden Plas did come with a tinted anti-glare band across the top of its screen. The two V8s came with the sunroof only optional on cheaper models, and both of them had alloy wheels as standard; the 2600S and 2300S had stainless steel trims; and the 2300 had a new grey plastic trim which looked considerably more expensive than the one it replaced!

The interior transformation was even more successful. While the 2300 kept its old-style seats in just two shades of brown cropped velour, the 2300S, 2600S and 3500SE could be had with no fewer than four colours of pinstripe velvet upholstery. The Vanden Plas meanwhile came with either light or dark brown leather, or with hairline woven velvet as an option. The new seats on the 2300S and above all had an adjustable lumbar pad and a turnwheel recline adjustment. Instrument pods were now coloured to match the rest of the interior, and their switchgear was illuminated.

There were better carpets, bright door kick-plates bearing the Rover name, a leather-rimmed steering wheel, and a ram-air setting on the heater. Electric windows were fitted to the 2600S and both V8 models, and all cars with automatic transmission had a more solid and expensive-looking selector lever. Lastly, the Vanden Plas came with an electric sunroof, electrically-adjusted and electrically-heated door mirrors, a cruise control, four head restraints with detachable cushions, bright highlights on the facia and footwell overmats.

### The 1982-1986 models

The 1982 model-year started late for the SD1 range – in fact on January 20, 1982. That date marked another major turning point in SD1 history, when a facelifted range was introduced. Often known as the 'Series 2' range in the motor trade, this started off with the same five models as

before, plus a new entry-level 2000 variant. However, over the next few years, it went through a number of permutations.

The hierarchy of specification levels established for the 1981 models remained unchanged: the entry-level models had no letter after their engine size designation; next up were the S models; above those came SE types; and the Vanden Plas topped the range. So the 1982 model-year began with 2000, 2300, 2300S, 2600S, 3500SE and Vanden Plas models. From April that year, the arrival of the turbodiesel engine added the 2400SD Turbo designation (2.4 litres, S-level specification, Diesel, Turbocharged). These seven models were joined by two more in October 1982, as the SE trim became available with the 2.6-litre engine to make a 2600SE and the high-performance Vitesse was introduced. The next range realignment came in May 1984, when both the 2600SE and 3500SE were dropped, a new 2600 Vanden Plas variant was introduced, and the Vanden Plas EFi (with the Vitesse's engine) took over as the top model. These nine models were reduced to eight

An early 2600 engine equipped with twin SU HS6 carburettors. It offered good economy, but if neglected it could prove troublesome in later life.

95

when the 2400SD Turbo went out of production in 1985, and the remaining types continued until production stopped in early 1986.

The key styling features of the 1982 and later models were their large black polyurethane bumpers; their enlarged tailgate windows with a standard wash-wipe system; and their flush-fitting headlamps and all-amber corner-lamp lenses. A black air intake grille ran above the front bumper, and bright trim highlighted the headlamps, the bumpers on the S and higher specification levels, and the side bump-rubbers of the Vanden Plas, which had now moved down below the bodyside indentation. The S and higher specification levels also included a body-coloured front spoiler, which gave the cars a lower and more sporting appearance.

Other details had changed as well. With the Vanden Plas and SE trim levels came a flat-faced spoked alloy wheel, in natural metal finish on SEs and enamelled grey for the Vanden Plas. The S specification brought new stainless steel wheel covers, with black-painted 'petals', and the entry-level cars had the plastic trims first seen on the 1981-model 2300. The Denovo option had been abandoned, however. Poor wear characteristics of the early tyres had given the product a bad name, and in fact during the early 1980s Dunlop and Rover set up a scheme which allowed

owners of Denovo-shod cars to exchange their wheels for conventional ones.

SE and Vanden Plas trim levels brought twin coachlines, bronze tinted glass, mudflaps and spoiler-mounted fog lamps as standard. The Vanden Plas models had headlamp washers in large overriders, and the V8-engined models had a '3500' badge on their front wings, matching the existing

The most immediately obvious changes in the 1982 facelift were at the nose, where the headlamps were resited flush with the front panel, and large rubber bumpers stood above a stylish chin spoiler. This car also has the headlamp washers, standard only on top models but optional elsewhere.

Not everybody liked the side graphics on the original Vitesse, so they quickly became a 'delete option' and were then dropped altogether. This car is actually one of the rare automatic versions, although there is nothing to give that away in this picture.

This 1985-model 2600S carries the black badge plinth and blacked-out door handle frames introduced during 1984.

For 1985, the Vitesse was given a unique and deeper front spoiler, and exchanged its side graphics for a more practical bump-strip.

A revealing exposure of the SD1's body structure and mechanical layout, indicating the generous passenger and luggage accommodation and the considerable front overhang.

2600 style. Meanwhile, all cars had a new full-width silver badge plinth at the rear, and the finishing touch was a single-point windscreen washer outlet mounted on the scuttle instead of on the bonnet.

Upholstery was essentially the same as on the 1981 models, although the optional Vanden Plas hairline velvet trim was now standard on SEs and all cars had colour-keyed safety belts. Dominating the facia, a big new instrument binnacle lent a new air of solidity to the interior, while a revised steering wheel and a lidded storage box on the centre console made even entry-level SD1s seem plusher. The door trim mouldings were more solid than before, adding to the air of quality and bringing with them the much-missed traditional Rover feature of wood fillets on all except the entry-level cars. The S-specification brought light-coloured satin-finish fillets; the SE had burr walnut; and on the Vanden Plas the wooden door fillets were matched by burr walnut facings on the dashboard.

Steering column stalks had switched sides to suit the new ISO standards, and a trip computer was standard on Vanden Plas models and optional on others. Central

locking was standard with the S-level trim and above, and the SE and Vanden Plas trims included rear-seat reading lamps and a courtesy light delay. Electric aerials were the preserve of SE and Vanden Plas specifications, and only the Vanden Plas had a three-band radio-cassette, all the others having two-band types. Although a sunroof was now standard right across the range, it was electrically operated only on the Vanden Plas. This top trim level once again included electrically heated and adjusted door mirrors; Vanden Plas front seats also had map pockets in their backs.

Very few exterior changes were made over the remaining four years of SD1 production although there were several interior changes and specification upgrades. As far as the ordinary models were concerned – the Vitesse is dealt with separately – the 1984 model-year brought the first changes, as the door handle surrounds switched from bright metal to black plastic. Black badge plinths and reshaped door mirror bases followed in May 1984, and radio aerials disappeared in July 1985 when the rear window heating element was wired in to substitute. The final exterior change came in

January 1986, when small square repeater flashers (already specified for some export markets) were added to the front wings of all models.

Interior trim went through rather more changes. A carpeted kick-panel was added to the door trims on SE and Vanden Plas models for the 1983 season, and for 1984 all door trims had a colour-contrasted panel. Upholstery on the Vanden Plas cars was leather until the end of the 1984 season, with Raschelle knitted fabric being that year's option; woven hairline velvet was the option for 1982 and 1983. For 1985 and 1986, box velvet was standard, while leather became an extra-cost option.

Hairline velvet was always the SE specification unless the optional leather was ordered. The S trim was pinstripe velvet until May 1984, and then took over the SE's hairline velvet for 1985 and 1986, after a few months when shadowstripe and plain velvet was standard. Entry-level 2000 and 2300 models had cropped velour upholstery in brown for 1982 and 1983, Shetland Tweed for 1984, and plain velvet for 1985 and 1986, again after a brief interlude in summer 1984 when pinstripe velvet was specified.

Sunroofs were manual except on Vanden Plas models and with the S trim for 1985 and 1986, while mirrors were electric only on the Vanden Plas until they were standardized across the range, again for 1985 and 1986. Central locking was standard on all models except the entry-level 2000 and 2300, and from mid-1983 the original solenoid-operated type was replaced by a more reliable motorized type. Air conditioning was never standard in any model, but an improved variety was introduced for the 1984 model-year, and the ICE systems of all SD1s were upgraded in May 1984. Bronze-tinted glass, initially associated with SE and Vanden Plas trim levels, was standardized across the range for the 1983 and subsequent model-years.

The high-performance Vitesse was the flagship of the SD1 range until the Vanden Plas EFi replaced it as the most expensive variant in May 1984. Its name (appropriately, the word is French for 'speed') was new to Rover and came from the Triumph stable; Rover had originally wanted to call the car a Rover Rapide, but Aston Martin-Lagonda refused to give up their rights to the Rapide name.

The original Vitesse was easy to recognize by its spoked alloy wheels with Pirelli P6 205/60 VR 15 low-profile tyres, its big black polyurethane rear spoiler (strictly unnecessary for road use, in fact), a black rear badge plinth and by black aerodynamic fairings ahead of the rear wheelarches. It also had Vanden Plas-type headlamp washers and came in a restricted range of colours. As announced in October 1982, the car had huge decals along the lower flanks bearing its name. These met with mixed reactions, however, and by the beginning of 1983, customers could ask for them to be left off.

Changes to the exterior generally followed those on the other SD1 models, but the 1985-model Vitesses (introduced in October 1984) were facelifted. The side decals and rear wheelarch fairings disappeared, and Vanden Plas-style bump rubbers were fitted along the flanks. In addition, a unique front spoiler, developed for the factory racers, was added. As this had no provision for fog lamps,

The VM turbodiesel in the 2400SD Turbo was installed with a backward tilt.

Top of the range at the end was the Vanden Plas EFi, available only with automatic transmission.

those items – standard since 1976 on V8 cars – were deleted.

The Vitesse interior specification was also special, with special sports front seats and upholstery in two-tone grey velvet. Wood trim was initially the S-level satin-finish type, although it changed to burr walnut in May 1984. A trip computer and four-speaker radio-cassette system were fitted from the beginning, and air conditioning was always an option. The sunroof was manually operated as standard, the mirrors were always electric and the windscreen carried an anti-glare band across its top.

**Powertrain and 'chassis' elements**
The basic suspension layout of the SD1 was determined by Spen King and laid out in detail by Gordon Bashford. It used space-efficient Triumph-style MacPherson struts at the front, with a coil-sprung torque-tube 'live' axle at the rear. Technically, this latter was a retrograde step after the sophistication of the P6's De Dion rear suspension, but King's hands were tied by the need to minimize the car's

manufacturing costs. The rear axle was located by trailing arms and a Watts linkage, and rubber bushes were used extensively to build in the compliance which King believed so important in any suspension system. The V8-engined cars, 2600s and 2400SD Turbos always had Boge Nivomat ride-levelling damper struts on the rear axle, but the others had ordinary telescopic dampers.

Brakes, too, looked like a step backwards from the P6's advanced all-disc system, as the discs on the front wheels were matched by drums at the rear. The Vitesse and Vanden Plas EFi models had ventilated discs with four-piston calipers for improved stopping power, although they still retained the rear drums. Power-assistance was, of course, standard from the beginning, right across the range, and the hydraulic circuit was split front to rear and had a pressure-limiting valve in the rear line. The steering did represent an advance over the P6 type, however, with a rack-and-pinion system which could be either unassisted (in the 2000, 2300 and early 2600 models) or power-assisted (in all other models, and optionally in those three). In either case, it gave excellent feel and very precise control which, allied to the SD1's wide track, made the car feel very stable at speed.

For the manual transmission models, the designers came up with a modular gearbox which could be made with either four forward speeds or five, the fifth being an overdrive. This was called the LT77, the letters standing for Leyland Transmissions and the 77 showing that there were 77mm between its mainshaft and layshaft centres. The four-speed version was used only in the 2300 before 1981; all other SD1s had the five-speed, which was also an extra-cost option for the 2300. These five-speed gearboxes were all essentially the same, although a taller overdrive fifth was introduced with the facelifted 1982 models, and the 2400SD Turbo always had a unique and slightly shorter fifth-gear ratio. Vitesse models also had a strengthened version of the gearbox, with the shot-peened gears also used in LT77s supplied to Jaguar for the XJ6. The only SD1 not to have the LT77 gearbox was the automatic-only Vanden Plas EFi, introduced in 1984.

Automatic transmissions were available on every SD1 variant except for the 2400SD Turbo. In the beginning, the 2300, 2600 and 3500 all used the three-speed Borg-Warner type 66, an improved version of the type 65 seen in the final P6s. However, this was replaced across the range by a GM180 three-speed transmission towards the end of 1982. The Vitesse was not initially available with an automatic transmission, but customer demand persuaded Rover to introduce an automatic option in January 1984. The option was short-lived, however, and had disappeared by the end of the year, when customers who wanted the combination of the high-performance engine and automatic transmission had turned to the Vanden Plas EFi.

As for engines, there were six basic types in the SD1. Top of the range was always the 3.5-litre V8, initially in carburettor form and later with fuel injection; next were the two six-cylinders, with 2.6-litre and 2.3-litre capacities. From 1982, there was the Austin O-series 2-litre four-cylinder for the 2000, and slightly later in that year came the 2.4-litre turbocharged four-cylinder diesel, bought in from VM Motori in Italy.

The 3.5-litre V8 had been developed from its P6B application to have a higher rev limit, improved valving, and more efficient exhaust arrangements. Its air intake also incorporated BL's award-winning air temperature control system for faster warm-up. With the twin SU carburettors fitted up to the end of 1981, it developed 155bhp – some 12bhp more than the superseded P6B's V8. Twin Solexes with an automatic choke were fitted between 1982 and 1984, and thereafter twin SUs were specified again, this time with electronic mixture control. The 1982 and later engines were rated at 157bhp – although the difference was purely academic. After 1978, incidentally, responsibility for the manufacture and development of the V8 passed to Land Rover Ltd, who then sold completed engines to Rover for the SD1.

Staple engine of the SD1 range was always the V8, although the 2.6-litre six-cylinder ran it a very close second on popularity. An early SU-carburetted V8 is seen here in cutaway display form.

In theory, just 500 'twin-plenum' Vitesse models were built, although that number is disputed. The engine – easily recognizable by the two intake hoses running to the plenum chamber – offered more torque than the standard injected V8, but no more power.

Rover had been experimenting with fuel injection systems since the late 1960s, and the first production applications on the V8 engine were seen in 1979, when the SD1 was introduced to the USA. The Lucas injection system then was tuned to control exhaust emissions rather than for power, but it was not long before Rover started looking at a high-performance version of the SD1, using a retuned fuel injection system. A higher compression ratio and improved gas flow from reshaped valves with modified stems helped boost maximum power to 190bhp and gave a meaty torque delivery which turned the Vitesse into a worthy match for the high-performance saloons then coming from Mercedes, BMW and Audi. This same engine was later also used in the Vanden Plas EFi, which combined the top performance with the highest equipment levels. Right at the end of production, an even more highly tuned 'twin-plenum' version of the fuel-injected V8, derived from the Lotus-developed racing engine, was made available; power outputs and even numbers made are in dispute, however.

The two six-cylinder engines were developed by Triumph under the codename of PE146. Work had started on them in 1970, when they had been planned as a simple OHC conversion of the existing Triumph 2-litre and 2.5-litre sixes which could trace their ancestry back to the 1961 Standard Vanguard Six. However, by the time they were signed-off for production in 1973, they had very little in common with the older engine, having taken on a belt-driven overhead camshaft and elements of the ingenious valve-gear used in the Dolomite Sprint engine. By retaining a common 81mm bore but using different crankshafts and pistons, the design team was able to create both 2.3-litre and 2.6-litre engines with a high degree of component commonality, which of course saved manufacturing costs. Other sizes were theoretically possible, but were never needed.

Both the sixes started out with twin SU HS6 carburettors, both switched to HIF44s in 1982, and had HIF44Es with electronic mixture control between 1984 and 1986. None of this affected their power outputs, which remained at 123bhp for the smaller engine and 136bhp for the larger throughout. Fuel economy – which had enjoyed a high priority among the original design targets – was remarkably good, particularly on the 2.6-litre engine which became deservedly the more popular of the two. However, both had certain inherent design weaknesses which caused expensive trouble when they reached second and third owners who were less scrupulous about servicing, and as a result the six-cylinders earned themselves a bad reputation.

The 2-litre four-cylinder was incorporated into the SD1 programme in the early 1980s, as Jaguar-Rover-Triumph broke up and Rover became aligned with the Austin-Morris volume cars division. The engine was in fact an uprated, twin-carburettor, version of the one already seen in the Morris Ital – an ancestry which has not endeared it to diehard Rover enthusiasts. Nevertheless, it offered adequate performance, and allowed the SD1 to compete quite effectively with 2-litre Ford Granadas, Volvos, Citroëns and Renaults.

Last – and very much least in the estimation of many British SD1 enthusiasts – there was the four-cylinder turbodiesel, the first diesel engine ever to go into a production Rover saloon. High diesel fuel taxation had tended to discourage the development and sales of diesel engines in Britain, and as a result British car manufacturers were simply not prepared for the wave of interest in diesel which swept the European continent after the 1979 oil crisis. If Rover was to compete effectively across the Channel, it clearly needed diesel engines, and so a strategy was quickly drawn up in 1979. For the longer term, nothing less than a diesel version of the 3.5-litre V8 was planned (although the joint project with Perkins was abandoned at the end of 1983), and in order to get a diesel Rover into production in the short term, BL turned to the Italian VM company which was already building diesel engines for Alfa Romeo and others.

The engine VM supplied for the SD1 was the 2.4-litre HR492, an overhead-valve design with four separate indirect-injection cylinder heads, a KKK exhaust-driven turbocharger and a Bosch injection system. It was canted slightly backwards in the SD1's engine bay, with hydraulic front mountings to damp out vibration. On its launch, the 2400SD Turbo was the fastest diesel saloon available in

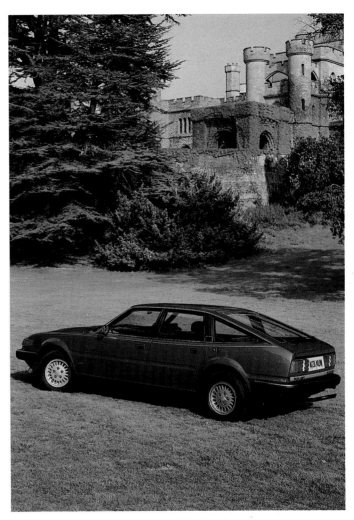

A 1985-model SD1 with the 2.6-litre engine shows off the alloy wheels and enlarged rear window characteristic of the later cars.

The four-cylinder 2000 engine always looked rather lost in the engine bay of the SD1.

Britain, with a top speed of just over 100mph and acceleration broadly similar to that of the SD1 2000. However, it was much more expensive than a 2000, and without the incentive of cheaper diesel fuel, British buyers failed to see the point of the car. Sales in continental Europe were quite strong – particularly in Italy – and they helped to build the Rover name in a market where it had previously meant very little. Nevertheless, the Rover car engineers never were completely happy with the VM installation, and warned their colleagues at Land Rover to take extra care when fitting the more powerful intercooled version of the engine to the Range Rover a few years later!

**Overseas variations and oddities**
Rover had started to produce special variants of its cars to suit overseas markets with the P5, and the process had continued with the P6. By the time of the SD1, increasingly divergent export requirements demanded a corresponding diversity of special models. In some cases, it was possible simply to mix and match, as Rover did with the 2000S which was sold only in Italy. This had the smallest 2-litre engine because taxation was punitive on larger petrol engines in Italy, but combined it with the mid-level S trim

specification. However, in other cases, much more major changes were needed.

Such was the case with a version of the 3500 designed for the US and Canadian markets – the scene of previous Rover sales disasters. The car was announced in June 1980 as a 1981 model, and received enthusiastic press reviews. Essentially similar to the home-market V8-S, it had large impact-absorbing bumpers and four round headlamps, and under its bonnet was an emissions-controlled, 133bhp fuel-injected version of the V8 engine. This gave a maximum speed of 116mph and a 0-60mph time of 10 seconds. Sadly, fewer than 1,000 cars had been sold before BL decided to pull out of the North American market when the strength of the pound against the dollar made the cars uneconomical to sell without an unacceptable rise in showroom prices.

The Australian market also took special versions of the 3500, the only model available there. Local regulations demanded an emissions-controlled engine from the time of SD1's Australian launch in October 1978, and so the cars

The interior of the early cars looked inviting enough, but material quality was disappointing, and fit and finish were often poor. This is an early 3500 automatic, with manual window winders – the one by the driver's leg was almost inaccessible on the move.

had a low-compression, 136bhp version of the V8 with Zenith-Stromberg carburettors, an air injection pump and an exhaust gas recirculation system. From mid-1981, the Australian SD1 became a 3500SE with a 142bhp version of the US models' fuel-injected engine, this powering all Australian SD1s until sales stopped at the end of 1985.

South Africa also had its own special SD1s, in this case locally assembled from kits sent out by Rover. Tax regulations ensured that the South African cars also had a high proportion of locally-manufactured parts – which included unique engines and interior trims. Although the SDE (3500 automatic) and SDS (3500 five-speed) had broadly familiar mechanical specifications, the SD (basic 2600) and SDX (high-specification 2600) had a locally-built 2,623cc six-cylinder engine called the R6, which was derived from the four-cylinder engine in the Morris Marina. This had 110bhp and gave the cars acceleration and a maximum speed broadly equivalent to those of the British-built 2000. The first South African cars were built in 1978, and the 1982 facelift echoed its UK equivalent, although the cars never took on the polyurethane bumpers but stayed with the rubber-faced stainless steel type of 1981-specification V8 models.

India, too, had special SD1s – although rather later than other markets. During 1985, Standard Motor Products Ltd of Madras began to assemble a car they called the Standard 2000, which used SD1 body shells (shipped out CKD from Britain) and a locally-designed gearbox, rear axle, and 2-litre engine. When SD1 production ended in Britain, the body tooling was sold to Standard and shipped out to Madras. The Standard 2000 became India's most expensive and prestigious saloon, but sales were slow and production stopped in 1989.

Overseas markets were not the only recipients of SD1s with unusual specifications. The SD1 quickly became a favourite with British Police forces as a motorway patrol car, and Rover tackled this market by offering a special Police specification. Generally speaking, this came with the V8 engine in standard tune (although some forces also bought 2600s), a strengthened five-speed gearbox, and the least well-equipped bodyshell (lacking sunroof, central

Improved upholstery materials and better fit and finish characterized the 1981 models. This is a 3500SE.

locking and electric windows, and with rubber matting instead of carpet in the boot). Many later examples also had the ventilated disc brakes with four-piston calipers which went into production on the Vitesse.

Lastly, the SD1 did spawn two interesting variations, neither of which entered production. Right from the beginning, BL management had wanted an estate variant of the SD1 to replace the estate variants of the Triumph 2000 and 2500 saloons. A prototype was built in 1976 by Michelotti in Turin on the basis of an early 3500, and then a second car was built by Carbodies in Britain. However, it soon became clear that the standard hatchback saloon offered versatility close to that of an estate, and so the project was abandoned. The other SD1 variant was a convertible, built by SMC Engineering of Bristol in 1980 without factory involvement. The market which SMC anticipated in the USA did not materialize when Rover stopped selling SD1s across the Atlantic, and the single left-hand drive 3500 convertible eventually found its way to Belgium.

The facelifted cars had a completely revised instrument panel, a new centre console and new door trims and upholstery. This interior belongs to a Vitesse – the only model to have the two-tone grey cloth seats.

Wood and leather in this left-hand-drive 2600 Vanden Plas hark back to the Rovers of old. This was what the customers had wanted from the beginning.

# CHAPTER 7

# The Rovers that got away

## What might have been

### Stillborn prototypes

#### M-Type

Towards the end of the Second World War, it seemed clear to Spencer Wilks that in the economic depression which was bound to follow, demand for the medium-sized cars which were Rover's stock-in-trade would fall off and be replaced by a demand for cheaper, smaller cars. To ensure the Company's long-term survival, therefore, he had approved a plan to produce a 6hp car. Prototypes of the M-type (M for Miniature) were built and tested in 1945-46, but the car never saw production. The Government emphasis on medium-sized cars as desirable exports, their one-maker/one-model policy, and above all their change to a flat-rate motor taxation system, all conspired to kill it off.

The baby Rover, designed by Gordon Bashford with styling by Harry Loker under Maurice Wilks' guidance, sat on a 77in wheelbase, and was powered by a 28hp 699cc version of the four-cylinder IOE engine. Steel shortages had been foreseen and both the platform-chassis and the body were therefore fabricated from light alloy. Despite its small size, the car was a full four-seater, capable of around 60mph. Performance and handling were good and the vehicle could have been every bit as good as the early Morris Minor, although it must be admitted that styling was rather less successful, the body having heavy rear quarters and generally looking like a rather overweight Fiat 500. The front grille and headlamp arrangement was echoed on early clay models for both the P3 and P4.

Although an open version was under consideration, the three prototypes all had two-door closed bodies. One of them survived into the 1960s in the hands of Jess Worster, Director of Rover's Tyseley Works, and an engine has since been discovered and preserved for the Heritage collection.

#### Road Rover

The Road Rover was always an odd project in that its precise purpose never seemed to be clearly defined. It grew originally out of the Land-Rover as a rather more refined two-wheel-drive variant of the station wagon, using a P4 car chassis. The first prototype was built in 1952 and was christened 'The Greenhouse' because of its basic, Land-Rover-derived styling. Several more prototypes to similar specification were built until a rethink in 1955 attacked the problem from the other end, as it were, and redefined the aim as a rugged two-wheel-drive estate car, closer in concept to the cars than to the Land-Rover. With a completely new body, based heavily on contemporary Chevrolet styling and apparently using some saloon car parts, the first Series 2 Road Rover was built in spring 1956. Like the earlier prototypes, this had a modified P4 car chassis and a 1,997cc P4 60 engine, but later cars in the prototype series had the 2,286cc Land-Rover petrol engine.

Production plans were ambitious; besides the basic two-door Station Wagon, a two-door Saloon, a Van and a Pickup with either cab or canvas hood were drawn up, and work began on a four-door Station Wagon. Production was scheduled to begin in early 1958, but was put off until autumn 1959, then July 1960, and finally the Road Rover project collapsed about the middle of 1959. No-one quite knows why, but it seems probable that there were three main factors: the whole project had become over-complicated, the exact sales area had still not been fully defined, and Solihull had quite enough other work to do on the P6 project. Several years later, the Road Rover concept would re-emerge in a much-refined form as the Range Rover.

## T3

The T3 was actually the fourth gas turbine prototype, and was the first such Rover not to use a production body/chassis structure. Based on a box-section chassis-frame with a 94in wheelbase, it had a two-door, two-seater, fixed-head coupe body made of glass-reinforced polyester resin with local steel reinforcing members inserted at the moulding stage.

Following the exhaust gas dispersal problems encountered with the front-engined T2, the 2S/100 turbine engine was

The M-type was a baby car which would have been built to traditional Rover standards of quality.

MWD 716 was one of the first series of Road Rover prototypes, and is similar to the vehicle now owned by the Heritage Collection

108

T3, the four-wheel-drive gas turbine coupe, is now preserved by Heritage

mounted at the rear. It produced around 110bhp to give this 19¼cwt car a top speed in the region of 115mph. The transmission dispensed with the T2A's conventional gearbox and reverted to the JET 1 pattern in which the engine performed the function of a torque convertor, so that all the driving could be done on a single ratio. A simple change lever selected reverse, which had exactly the same gearing as forward.

Chassis engineering was by Spen King and incorporated many of the ideas which he and Gordon Bashford would later put into the P6. The rear suspension was a De Dion layout with fixed-length drive-shafts and a Watt linkage, a sliding-joint arrangement being employed to take care of variations in track. Inboard Dunlop disc brakes were fitted front and rear, with rack-and-pinion steering and coil-spring-and-wishbone independent front suspension. To aid traction and roadholding, a four-wheel drive layout was used.

The T3, as a bodyless test-bed, began testing on January 16, 1956. It first ran as a complete car at MIRA on September 16, and was displayed at the London Motor Show later that year, although there was never any intention that it should become a production model. It remained a

development car for a number of years – work concentrating on the heat-exchangers Rover hoped would reduce the high fuel consumption which handicapped all the gas turbine cars – and it is now retained by the British Motor Industry Heritage Trust.

### P6BS/P9

The P6BS owed its inception to the exciting possibilites which the ex-Buick V8 engine opened up in the mid-1960s, and indirectly to William Martin-Hurst's enthusiasm for sporting cars and the success of the Rover-BRM gas turbine car. Quite different from the normal run of Rover projects, it was a mid-engined three-seater sports car drawn up by Spen King and Gordon Bashford, using an all-steel welded body and a number of P6 running components, hence its P6 designation, plus B for Buick and S for Sports.

The heart of the design was a Buick V8 engine, modified with parts from its Rover derivative and fitted with big 2in SUs to give around 185bhp. Mounted back-to-front and offset slightly to the right, it left room for a third passenger seat alongside. Drive was taken through a four-speed gearbox to the rear wheels, which had a semi-independent De Dion setup. The car's light weight, low build and wide

This styling studio mock-up shows the impressive lines of the big P8 saloon. Just visible behind is a Range Rover styling buck.

track allied to the mid-engined layout gave staggeringly good roadholding and handling and top speed was in the region of 140mph. Without a doubt, production cars could have been even faster, and the use of P6 running-gear convinced Rover that the car could have been sold very cheaply indeed.

The roadgoing P8 prototypes were badged as 'Mantelays' to confuse industry and press spies. Photograph by Alan Milstead; badge from the Geoff Kent Collection.

The P6BS prototype, with the P9 styling model proposed by David Bache's team. Although the car would probably have become an Alvis, it bears Rover badging here. There are still many who bitterly regret that it never went into production.

NMT 396E was built up during 1966 and registered for road use in the early part of 1967. Early plans had been to put it into production under the badge of Rover's Alvis subsidiary and most of the testing of the prototype was done by Alvis. By 1968, however, it was clear that the car would not go into production and British Leyland management lent it out to various motoring journals for road-test as an interesting might-have-been. The overwhelmingly enthusiastic reviews which these magazines printed may well have been a factor in the 1969 decision to reconsider the car for production. As the chunky, functional body style with its simple single-curvature panels had never been intended by Bashford and King as a production design, David Bache's styling team were instructed to redraw the car. The project had got as far as a full-size mock-up when Jaguar's Sir William Lyons heard about it. When he learned that Rover intended to sell this new P9 at several hundred pounds below the cost of an E-type, he used all the influence he had on the British Leyland Board to get the project killed off. Less than two years later, he would do the same to ensure that the P8 did not spoil the market for Jaguar's XJ saloons; sadly, Rover had no representative on the British Leyland Board who commanded the same respect as Sir William.

Although an early picture of the P6BS being built in the jig shop at Solihull shows it with Rostyle wheels, it was fitted with Minilites when Rover lent it to the motoring journals. The Rover 2000 wheels and hubcaps with which it has latterly been seen scarcely do justice to the design, and one is tempted to suspect that their fitting may have been intended to detract from the appeal of a vehicle which should, without any doubt, have been built. The unique prototype now forms part of the Heritage collection, where it is kept company by a splendid one-eighth scale model of the Bache-designed P9.

## P8

The P8 was the second of the two major disappointments in Rover's history after the British Leyland takeover. It had first begun to take shape in 1963 as a luxury-market successor to the P5; design work had become very serious two years later when the V8 engine became available, and the British Leyland Board gave it the go-ahead in 1968. From the first, the P8 had been conceived as a Mercedes rival, but it gradually became apparent that it would also be a Jaguar rival. As British Leyland were unwilling to risk a head-on clash between the two marques the Rover had to go. So go it did, in March 1971, less than six months before its scheduled launch date and after millions of pounds had already been spent on production tooling.

Few people would disagree that Sir William Lyons' XJ saloon was a much more graceful creation than David Bache's heavy, chunky P8, but the Rover design certainly had an impressive appearance and would no doubt have been tidied up for production. At one stage, gullwing doors had been seriously considered, but the final design approved for production was a conventional four-door saloon. Basic and detail design were settled in 1968, but by the time the first prototypes were built in 1970 the car had become larger and heavier than its progenitor Spen King would have wished. By then, of course, he had been spirited away to look after the Triumph operation.

The P8 used a base-unit structure generally similar to that of the P6, to which light-alloy skin panels were attached. It had a 108½in wheelbase, with a coil-spring De Dion rear suspension incorporating self-levelling struts, which represented a refinement of the P6 layout. The front suspension was of double-wishbone type, mounted on a tubular subframe which could move fore-and-aft on rods running through the tubes and was bolted at the front to a body crossmember and at the rear to the member carrying the wishbone link pivots. Power-assisted rack-and-pinion steering was to be standard, together with full-power high-pressure disc braking.

The model line-up and model names chosen remain unclear, but some of the seven prototypes ran a 4.4-litre V8 engine mated to automatic transmission, while the other cars had the familiar 3.5-litre power unit. A manual gearbox would have been available alongside the automatic option. At least one mock-up was badged as a Rover 4000, and a noteworthy feature of the design was the use of polyurethane impactable bumpers front and rear, which would have been painted in the body colour. Some of the prototypes were later used to test SD1 components, and only one (TXC 160J, the seventh prototype) survived unmodified. This automatic-transmission car, which was regrettably vandalized while in store at Longbridge, is now the property of Heritage. This car appears never to have had any badging, but some other P8 prototypes wore Mantelay badges to mislead the curious.

Interestingly enough, many of the items developed for the P8 reappeared in other Rover models. The box-pleated seating was used in the later P6s, and some features of the interior were retained at the insistence of Lord Stokes, then Chairman of British Leyland, for the early SD1 models. The controversial skeletal bonnet badge of the first SD1s had been drawn up originally for the P8 (it was also proposed for the P9), and the SD1's 'clover leaf' wheel trim was also first seen on a P8. As for the 4.4-litre engine, it found a home in the Australian Leyland P76 range and in Australian Leyland Terrier trucks.

Finally, not a prototype, but a Rover SD1 with quite a few performance-enhancing differences. The 3500 became a popular motorway patrol car, and this 1979 example – belonging to London's Metropolitan Police – is equipped with Minilite alloy wheels to improve brake cooling.

# CHAPTER 8

# Racing and rallying Rovers

## Competition cars from Rover

Although a number of 'specials' based on Rover mechanical parts were built by enthusiasts for trials and club racing in the years immediately after the war, undoubtedly the best-known was the Rover Special built for their own amusement by three of Rover's young engineers, Spen King, Peter Wilks and George Mackie. No-one could deny that the car had a distinguished career in club racing in its early years and, indeed, it continues to perform well in Historic racing events at the time of writing. Nevertheless, even greater interest attaches to its mechanical development over the years. Since it was built in 1948, the car has used a number of fascinating cast-off Rover prototype components and has also indirectly served as a test-bed for many of the ideas which King and Wilks put into Rover production cars of the 1950s and 1960s.

The car's first successes in 1949 attracted a limited amount of official approval from the Rover Company, but it always remained essentially a private venture, and until they became too deeply involved with the Marauder project, King, Wilks and Mackie raced it themselves. They were joined during 1949 by Jack Gethin, of the Birmingham Rover distributors, who took his turn at the wheel and provided in return both finance and workshop space. It was Gethin's firm which Peter Wilks would later join before returning to Rover after the failure of his own Marauder Car Company. Although other drivers used the car during the 1950s, it remained the property of its original owners until some time in the late 1960s, when it was sold to Frank Lockhart, its regular driver since 1963. Needless to say,

King, Wilks and Mackie always retained a fatherly interest in their 'baby'!

The chassis of the Rover Special was the prototype of what became the P3 chassis, designed just before the war by Adrian Lombard. The car also had prototype P3 IFS, and a four-cylinder prototype IOE engine of around 1.2 litres. By the time Rover agreed to part with it, it had already covered some 110,000 miles, having run throughout the war in a Rover 10! King, Wilks and Mackie shortened the chassis, fitted quarter-elliptic springs at the rear and lowered the front suspension, changed the axle ratio and added a single-seater body made by John Griffiths, which has subsequently been altered very little. Total weight was around 14cwt.

The car was first raced with its original engine bored out to 1.5 litres, but for the 1949 season it was given a discarded prototype 2,103cc P3 engine, which was sleeved down to 1,996cc (with a bore of 63.5mm) in order to get under the 2-litre barrier in force for Formula 2 events. Power was boosted by the use of triple SU carburettors, on a manifold similar to that seen on the triple-SU P3 75 cars and later on the Marauder 100, which was of course another Wilks-King-Mackie collaboration. With a compression ratio of 12:1, the engine was prone to head gasket failures, and an intriguing system of bolts was devised to ensure that the head stayed on. Inevitably, by this time Jack Swaine was helping out on engine development! The Rover gearbox – also said to have been a prototype – was discarded at the same time in favour of an ENV preselector unit of the type then familiar on the

These two photographs show the Rover Special as it was in 1982. The P3-type IFS can be seen in the front view.

racing circuits.

Axle development continued during 1949, and the differential was removed in order to obtain better sprint times. More significant, however, was the fitting in the winter of 1949 of a De Dion axle, still without a differential. Experience with this axle/suspension layout in the Rover Special led Spen King and Peter Wilks many years later to go for a De Dion rear end in the P6, and of course King's T3 gas turbine car and the P6BS coupe used De Dion

layouts. It is no coincidence, either, that the P6 had inboard disc brakes to reduce unsprung weight, as the Rover Special employed inboard brakes – albeit drums – for precisely the same reason.

In 1950, a prototype P4 90 engine was acquired for the car. It was simply an over-bored 75 unit of the type tried experimentally before the 'spread-bore' design was adopted. A special short-throw (78.75mm) crankshaft was ordered from Laystall and fitted, so that the capacity would still be under 2 litres. The 1,993cc engine was run on the test-bed with six Amal carburettors, but as most of the owners' enthusiasm and spare time was by now going into the Marauder venture, the engine was never actually put into the car.

Gerry Dunham (of Dunham and Haines, the Luton Rover agents) drove the car in some International events during the early 1950s, and these qualified it for the Historic section of VSCC events in which it now competes. Dunham replaced the 1,996cc engine with a P4 75 unit bored out to 2.4 litres, which was almost certainly in fact a Marauder 100 2,390cc engine, but by the time Frank Lockhart took over the Special in 1963, the 1,993cc engine was in the car. Unfortunately, the special crankshaft wrecked itself two years later, and at Spen King's suggestion an early 75 crank went in with 90 pistons to give the 2,638cc of the original prototype engine. A compression ratio of 9:1 was higher than the original, however. This engine ran its bearings in 1968, and was temporarily replaced by a P5 3-litre unit, wearing another triple-carburettor manifold – this time the prototype designed by Raymond Mays for the 3-litre several years earlier! Yet another engine swop took place in 1977, when a 2.6-litre unit was installed, again with the Mays manifold. An errant con-rod bolt wrote off this engine the following year, and so the earlier 2,638cc engine was rebuilt and reinstalled, fitted with the original (1949) triple-carburettor manifold. Thus the car remains today.

The Rover Special, of course, was rather separate from the mainstream of Rover engineering and policy. The Company did not actually put together a works team for serious competition in motor sport until the early 1960s, although they had sponsored several factory entries in the genteel British concours and long-distance road rallies of the 1930s.

Rover's Competitions Department was William Martin-Hurst's idea. Promoted in 1960 from Production Director to Managing Director, he set about preparing the way for the new image which the Company would need for the 1960s and beyond. Primarily, that new image was all to do with the Rover 2000, which was still a long way from its launch date, and somehow the existing cars had to be made into heralds of this new high-performance vehicle. The answer seemed to Martin-Hurst to lie in entering Rovers for motor sport – not circuit-racing, of course, but long-distance rallying of the type which would best show up the durability, reliability and high-speed cruising ability of the Company's newest product, the P5 3-litre.

The first step was to take a 3-litre to Africa and to hammer it up and down the continent for 15,000 miles in an extensive three-month tryout. This was followed by further testing at the Fighting Vehicle Research and Development Establishment at Bagshot, Surrey. The Board agreed that

One of the original 3-litre rally cars displays its competition equipment for the 1962 East African Safari. The door trim identifies this as a Mk IA model, and therefore as one of the locally-prepared cars.

677 DNX during the 1963 East African Safari, in which it was the only Rover to finish.

4 KUE was the car which took Roger Clark and Jim Porter to sixth place in the 1965 Monte Carlo Rally. It is seen here on the RAC Rally in 1964.

Martin-Hurst could go ahead with the 3-litre cars as rally entrants, but there was some initial caution about the enterprise: Rover simply gave official support to the first appearance of the 3-litres in rallying, and the team was actually entered for the East African Safari Rally in April 1962 by the Company's East African distributors, the Cooper Motor Corporation. Not until the cars had proved that they had some chance did Solihull set up its own Competitions Department, which was established with Ralph Nash at its head in July 1962. Nash continued to fulfil his duties as superintendent of the engineering workshops as well until Jim Porter assumed control of the Competitions Department during 1965 and he was able to return to his former job full-time. Although Nash knew nothing about rally-driving, he was fortunate in securing as his second-in-command Tony Cox, who did at least have experience of club rallying, and he was also able to assemble a team of expert mechanics from within his own department.

The object of the exercise was defined right from the start as being that the cars should finish – nobody expected them to win – and preparation was accordingly designed to keep them going at all costs. Nevertheless, when the engines were being blueprinted by the Experimental Department, the engineers there could not resist a few little touches like polished exhaust ports and ultra-tough valve springs, just to help things along! Exhausts, of course, were modified to give more bhp, and wiring (although not brake piping) was routed through the passenger compartment to make service attention easier.

There were actually two-and-a-half teams of 3-litre rally cars, the half a team being two of the four cars entered for the 1962 Safari which had been prepared locally, not by Solihull. Nevertheless, all four of the cars which would later form the first Rover team went to East Africa for the 1962 Safari, the two non-competitors acting as service and back-up vehicles. The problem of tracing which car was which is not made any easier by the fact that all the competing cars had to be registered locally (as KHD 262, 549, 550 and 551); all that can be established for certain is that the four cars which formed the team after this first rally had consecutive commission numbers in the Mk II series, and were then registered 676-679 DNX in July or August 1962.

Generally speaking, the Rover team drivers kept to one regular car, although the issue is complicated by the number of changes there were in that team of drivers! In the 1962 Safari, three of the cars were driven by local crews, but subsequently 676 DNX was normally driven by Johnny Cuff with John Howarth or John Baguley, 677 DNX was Bill Bengry's car and was shared with David Skeffington, 679 DNX belonged to Ken James and Mike Hughes, and 678 DNX was the 'guest driver' car, being piloted by Peter Riviere and Ronnie Adams and then Raymond Baxter and Ernest McMillan. In the summer of 1963, the DNX-registered cars were relegated to a second-division team, and put in regular appearances either as practice or service back-up vehicles, or as privately-entered cars prepared by the factory. 676 DNX was sold in October 1963 to Richard Martin-Hurst, the son of Rover's Managing Director, and was actively campaigned by him alongside the works team cars. 677 DNX was written off in a fairly spectacular accident during the 1964 Monte Carlo Rally, but the other two cars were still going strong as late as 1965, when they were driven by Army teams in the Scottish International Rally. Both were scrapped early in 1967, but the eventual fate of 676 DNX is unknown.

If the 3-litres did not exactly set the rallying world alight by their performance in the 1962 Safari, they did astound the motoring world by their reliability. Although two of the cars were put out of the running by accidents, the other two gained third and fifth places in the over-2,500cc class, coming 25th and 31st overall out of the 45 finishers (109 cars had started). Both were crewed by local teams, and an internal memorandum at Solihull made much of the comment from the Vincent father-and-son crew that the only problem they had encountered on their way to third place was when the car's cigar lighter had failed to function! The next rally in which the Rovers performed was the Liège-Sofia-Liège in the autumn, when all four DNX-registered cars ran as private entries prepared by the Rover Competitions Department. Two cars were eliminated by

Two competition cars were built with long-stroke V8 engines. JXC 808D was the first of these and it still exists, in private ownership.

accidents, Bill Bengry and David Skeffington came 18th and last of the 100 entrants to finish, but Ken James and Mike Hughes scored a magnificent class win, coming sixth overall. The same crew took 679 DNX to third place in the over-1,600cc Touring class and an 11th overall placing in the RAC Rally that winter, while the works cars as a whole took third place in the Manufacturer's Team Award. The DNX cars put in their last rallying appearance on Rover's behalf as a team for the East African Safari of April 1963. This proved to be an extraordinarily tough event and three of the cars were eliminated by accidents, but Bill Bengry and local driver G.E.Goby, who had piloted a 3-litre in the previous year's event, finished seventh and last of the 84 starters, gaining first place in their class. Not that there was much competition; they were the only large car to finish!

Meanwhile, the Competitions Department was preparing a second team of four 3-litres, this time Mk IIB models, but apparently fitted with the 'big crank' engine then under development for autumn 1964 introduction. These were registered in June as 996-999 GNX. 999 GNX was regularly crewed by Ken James and Mike Hughes, 997 GNX by Bill Bengry and Barry Hughes until they left Rover at the close

117

The 4.3-litre V8 racing engine.

works-entered 3-litres were put out by accidents. Ken James and Mike Hughes, however, achieved a class win and eighth place overall, while Bill Bengry and Barry Hughes took third place in the over-2,000cc class and 18th overall position. Five cars were entered for the RAC Rally in November, the four works cars including one of the older DNX vehicles, and the fifth entry being Tony Cox in the privately-prepared 998 GNX. As a publicity gimmick, the cars were entered without a service back-up, and expectations were not disappointed; all five finished, taking in addition third, fourth and fifth places in their class and coming third in the Manufacturer's Team Award.

1964 started off less well with two private entries in the Monte Carlo Rally, one of which went out after an accident, while Ken James and Mike Hughes finished the road section without loss of points, but were heavily penalized on the special stages, ending up 69th overall. Two of the four team entries finished the Acropolis Rally in May, with James and Hughes taking sixth overall and second in class, followed by Tony Cox and Willie Cave with 11th overall and fourth in class. Between them, with third position in the class and ninth overall placing, was the privately-entered 676 DNX of Richard Martin-Hurst, whose co-driver was the then barely-known Roger Clark. No 3-litres went in for the Alpine Rally in June, which was given over to the first competition appearance of the 2000s, and none of the Rovers – of which three were 3-litres, two entered by the works – finished in the Spa-Sofia-Liège later that year.

The 2000 was so much more obviously suited to competition work than the 3-litre that it was inevitable it should succeed the older model in the Rover team. Four 2000s were initially prepared at Solihull, but 1 KUE to 4 KUE were later to be joined by a variety of other cars which were technically privately-owned, even though they had been registered at Solihull. Most of these bore the XC registrations commonly found on Rover Company vehicles at the time, although an exception was 151 FLK, a very early 2000 with a registration number following on from the pre-production cars, which was campaigned by Tony Cox. From the start, two of the KUE cars ran prototype 2000TC engines, and eventually all the cars were TC-equipped.

of the 1963 rallying season, and the other two cars were driven variously by Johnny Cuff and Norman Baguley, Willie Cave and John Sprinzel or the Competitions Department's foreman Tony Cox, Ann Hall and Peter Riley, and Logan Morrison with Johnstone Syer. Their last appearance in the Rover team was in the 1964 Spa-Sofia-Liège, although private entrants used them in a number of rallies after that date. 999 GNX was sold to a dealer in May 1966 and its subsequent history is unknown, but the other three cars were broken up in April the following year.

Only 20 cars finished of the 120 entrants for the Liège-Sofia-Liège Rally of August 1963, and two of the four

Only two of the four works 2000s finished in their first rally, Ken James and Mike Hughes in a TC taking third in their class and ninth in the Grand Touring category, while Peter Riley's standard car achieved a third in class and fifth place in the Touring category. None of the 2000s finished in the Spa-Sofia-Liege, but Anne Hall and Pat Spencer managed a 16th overall plus third in the Ladies' section of the RAC Rally that November. All this was scarcely an auspicious start to the 2000s' competition career, but fortunately all was redeemed by Roger Clark's amazing performance in the 1965 Monte Carlo Rally when, driving 4 KUE with Jim Porter, he took a class win, first in the Production Touring Cars category and sixth place overall. In the excitement, nobody seemed to care that the other three works 2000s had failed to finish. Clark himself became an overnight star, and of course left Rover after the 1965 rallying season to go on to even greater things. Although the works 2000s put up some good performances subsequently, they were never to equal the 1965 Monte Carlo Rally success.

During 1965, the number of rallying 2000s proliferated. There were private entries prepared at Solihull in the Circuit of Ireland, the Welsh International Rally, the RAC Rally and the Scottish International Rally, with placings achieved by Logan Morrison and Johnstone Syer in the last-named (a class win and third overall), and by Tony Cox and David Fawcett in the Welsh event (third in class and 12th overall). Chris Knowles-Fitton and C.G. Nash also finished in this latter rally, in 32nd place overall. The works team entries were limited to the Acropolis, Alpine and RAC Rallies, and although none of the cars finished in the first of these, the results obtained in the other two enabled Rover to continue holding their heads high. In the Alpine Rally, Andrew Cowan and Brian Coyle came third overall and first in the Grand Touring category with a 2000TC, while of the standard cars, that driven by Roger Clark and Jim Porter claimed 10th overall and fourth in the Touring category, with Logan Morrison and Johnstone Syer in 16th place overall and fifth in the Touring category. Anne Hall and Pat Spencer achieved 22nd place overall and sixth in the

Rover's competition cars were not all based on production saloons. A collaborative effort with BRM resulted in a gas turbine-powered Rover-BRM appearing in the Le Mans 24-hours race in 1963 and – here – in 1965, when Graham Hill and Jackie Stewart brought the latest car home in 10th place despite an overheating engine, averaging 98.8mph and 13.5mpg. This car is now part of the BMIHT collection at Gaydon, Warwickshire.

Touring category, even after an unplanned excursion over a 40-foot slope near the end. Clark and Porter came 14th overall in the RAC Rally and were second in their class, while Morrison and Syer finished 17th overall and took third place in their class.

Rover announced a four-rally programme for 1966 – the Monte Carlo, Acropolis, Alpine and RAC events – with the possibility of supporting private entries in the Circuit of Ireland and Scottish International events. They duly sponsored the seven Rovers entered for the Monte Carlo in which, after a squabble over modifications which led to the Ford and BMC cars being disqualified, Jim Porter and Geoffrey Mabbs came 10th overall with the wire-wheeled TC registered JXC 8C – but then they pulled out of motor sport altogether. The ostensible reason was disenchantment after the Monte Carlo disqualification fiasco (although Rover's own cars had not been affected); the reason given to the public was the pressing need to devote the Engineering Department's time more fully to other commitments; but in fact it was becoming increasingly apparent at Solihull that in order to remain competitive in rallying it would be necessary to start thinking in terms of very much modified engines and lightweight bodyshells, and this was not what the Rover teams had been all about. Although the withdrawal was touted as 'temporary', the Competitions Department closed down for good. The fate of the rallying 2000s is not clear, although 4 KUE passed into the hands of Brian Terry, an engineer in the Experimental Department, who eventually resold it. Before letting it out of their sight, however, Rover had disguised the car by respraying it in white (it was originally Copperleaf Red) and, because Ralph Nash wanted to keep all the famous KUE registration plates, 4 KUE was re-registered as JXC 226C.

The closure of the Competitions Department was not the end of Rovers in competition, however. Four years later, Peter Browning, British Leyland's Competitions Manager, chose to campaign a Rover 3500 for the 1970 season and, despite both scepticism and obstruction from the Rover management, he was able – with Ralph Nash's help – to secure JXC 808D, which had started life in 1966 as one of the V8 development cars.

Development was carried out on behalf of BL by Roy Pierpoint and Bill Shaw, who fitted the car with a 4.3-litre Traco-Oldsmobile V8 (essentially a race-tuned version of the GM engine) and gave it a new lightweight racing body with flared wings and wheelarches. With four Weber carburettors the power output was 360bhp at 6,800rpm, so not surprisingly the standard Rover 2000 gearbox (mated to a Jaguar E-type differential) let the car down on more than one occasion! An American Muncie gearbox was then fitted and in the hands of Roy Pierpoint the car had a relatively successful season in club racing, its major success being first place in the 100-miles Saloon Car race at Silverstone.

JXC 808D was then sold off (and it still exists, in restored form) and work began on a Group 6 prototype car, initially for racing, but with a view to homologation as a Group 2 rally car. BL had not ruled out the possibility of a limited production run of special-equipment V8s, although Solihull management had considerable doubts about the idea! This second car was again the work of Pierpoint and Shaw, who fitted it with a similar big V8 to the first, although this time final development was carried out by BL's Competitions Department at Abingdon. In September 1971, the new car was entered for the 84-hours Marathon de la Route at the Nurburgring. Despite a strict rev limit of 4,500rpm, imposed because the car was relatively untried, the Rover shot away from the rest of the field on the first lap, and by the time it was forced to retire with severe propshaft vibration 16 hours later, it had an amazing three-lap lead over the rest of the field, headed by the works Porsches! Sadly, BL closed the Competitions Department before the car was able to prove its worth in any more races. Much later, Rovers would again fly the BL flag when the BL Motorsport Division's racing SD1s trounced the Ford opposition in the 1981 British Saloon Car Championship.

When the sport's governing body announced that the maximum engine capacity for Group 1 saloon racers would be raised from 3 litres to 3.5 litres for the 1980 season, the SD1 3500 became BL's natural choice as an entrant. BL Motorsport's Director, John Davenport, had a first car built by David Price Racing in the spring of 1979; testing began during October; and the first two racing SD1s contested a

Tom Walkinshaw and Win Percy raced this TWR-prepared Vitesse in the 1985 European Touring Car Championship.

few rounds of the 1980 Tricentrol British Saloon Car Championship in the hands of Jeff Allam and Rex Greenslade. As was by then customary, the cars had multiple sponsors, and wore the colours of Triplex, Esso and *Motor* magazine. Allam won at the saloon car race supporting the British Grand Prix, and the Rovers came first and second at the Donington Motor Show 200 race.

Tom Walkinshaw Racing had done some suspension work on the 1980 cars, and for 1981 TWR took over the full preparation of the cars from David Price Racing. Two cars raced that season, wearing *Daily Express* and Esso sponsors' colours, and despite a poor start to the season the Group 1 Rovers eventually won six of the 11 championship rounds, finishing first and second in no fewer than four of them. With TWR now firmly in charge of development – the company would prepare all the BL Motorsport Rovers until they were withdrawn at the end of 1986 – 1982 was another excellent season. That year running with sponsorship from Sanyo and Esso, the SD1s won six of the 11 BSCC rounds while Ford's Capris won the other five, and Jeff Allam won

the class for cars with engines from 2.5 to 3.5 litres' capacity. Meanwhile, the French drivers René Metge and Jean-Pierre Gabreau, and the Belgian driver Eddy Joosen were also showing well with SD1s in European events.

The BSCC regulations changed for 1983, and with them the cars. Group 1 was dropped, and the new Group A regulations brought the BSCC into line with the European Touring Car Championship. The three SD1s entered by Austin Rover Motorsport were based on the Vitesse, and featured 290bhp engines and Getrag five-speed gearboxes. Drivers Jeff Allam and Peter Lovett had the two Sanyo-sponsored cars, Steve Soper had the Hepolite-sponsored car, and the Rovers completely dominated the 1983 BSCC. However, opposing teams protested that the Rovers did not meet the Group A regulations – protests which were upheld by a tribunal which reported in 1984, and the Rovers were thus stripped of their championship title. Austin Rover refused to accept the findings, and in consequence withdrew the four works cars from the 1984 BSCC in mid-season. Nevertheless, 1984 remained a good year for the SD1 in competition, as privateer Andy Rouse won the BSCC driving an ICS-sponsored Vitesse prepared by his own company with input from Austin Rover.

Meanwhile, the Rovers had also started to appear in the events of the European Touring Car Championship. Their first races during 1983 were unsuccessful, as the cars were neither fast nor reliable enough for these longer-distance events. Austin Rover Fleet sponsored the two TWR-prepared ETCC cars during 1984, and later Gitanes sponsored a third, but reliability problems continued to dog the Rovers' efforts. Tom Walkinshaw himself, meanwhile, actually won the 1984 ETCC in a TWR-prepared Jaguar XJ-S.

Bastos and Texaco sponsored the three Vitesses which Austin Rover Motorsport entered in the 1985 ETCC, and this time Tom Walkinshaw and co-driver Win Percy were on the Austin Rover team. However, despite some extremely hard-fought events, the Rovers lost the championship to the surprisingly quick Volvo 240s. The same happened again in 1986, when the Rovers raced with the new Lotus-developed twin-plenum engine and the new deep front spoiler. These were the last works entries for the

SD1, although privateers had already begun to race Vitesses in the BSCC, and during 1987 did quite well in the renamed British Touring Car Championship. The last serious Vitesse entries were made in 1988, by which time Ford's Sierra Cosworth had begun to dominate the events.

The SD1 was also developed into a competent rally machine, and its career spanned the period from 1982 to 1985. The first Group 2 rally car was built over the winter of 1981-82, and with Unipart sponsorhip, it was entered by BL Motorsport in a few long-distance events during the spring of 1982, with former TR7 V8 rally driver Tony Pond at the wheel.

It was TWR who prepared the two Group A rallying Vitesses for 1983, although weak rear axles hindered their success. The following season was rather better, and the rallying SD1s saw some success in international rally events. Ironically, the SD1's final year in rallies was also its best, and during 1985 Tony Pond won the Shell Oils Open Championship in one of two Computervision-sponsored cars. For 1986, however, Austin Rover Motorsport switched to the Metro 6R4 as its rally contender, and the SD1s disappeared from view.

Brian Goff and Mike Stuart drive the Group A Computervision-sponsored Vitesse in the Tudor Webasto Manx Rally.

# CHAPTER 9

# Buying a Classic Rover

## The choice and the examination

When the first edition of this book appeared in 1983, enthusiasts of the marque tended to be divided into two camps: devotees of the pre-1950 wings-and-running-boards models and devotees of the P4s and P5s. As for the P6s, they were a little new to be counted as classic cars – although the subsequent rise of the P6 Rover Owners' Club has shown how highly they were, and still are, regarded. Today, the divisions have not really shifted, but a third group has grown up: those who like the P6s and SD1s.

However, one thing which has changed dramatically is the number of Classic Rovers in everyday use. Back in the early 1980s, many P4s and P5s were still in regular use, P6s were very common, and SD1s could still be bought new from the showrooms. Today, it is a rare sight indeed to see any one of these models on the road unless it is making its way to a classic car event of some kind on a summer weekend. And yet – ironically – the efforts of dedicated specialists have made it easier to find spares for most of the cars covered in this book than it was in the early 1980s.

### The choice

Enthusiasts looking for a wings-and-running-boards Rover built at Solihull must make their choice between the P2 (1946-47) and P3 (1948-49) models. By far the majority of these are, of course, six-light Saloons; four-light Sports Saloons are in rather poorer supply, and the 1947 Tourer is very rare indeed. None of these cars is in plentiful supply these days, and most examples have either been carefully restored or are complete basket-cases which have been off the road for years. There is therefore little point in going through their strengths and weaknesses in detail. Suffice it to say that the engines in the later P3 models offer rather better performance, although the P2s are generally more comfortable cars. The P3 also has an Achilles heel: when rust affects the rear of the body, major structural repairs are likely to be necessary to restore the strength needed for the rear springs to be safely located, as there is no separate chassis frame at the back of the car.

From the visual point of view, P4 models all look very similar, although there were actually five distinct body types: the Cyclops (1950-52 model years), the boxed headlight model with sloping boot (1952-54), the boxed headlight model with new boot and rear window (1955-56), the new wing model (1957-58), and the final version with revised bumpers and grille (1959-64). The early cars all had bench front seats covered in plain leather, which are both less comfortable and less durable than the pleated-leather type introduced at the same time as bucket front seats in 1956. Most comfortable are the final design with padded edge-rolls; reclining front seats became available in 1961 and fully-adjustable seats the following year. Bench seats were offered until the demise of the 95 and 110 in 1964. Boot space in all models is limited, but in the pre-1954 cars it is particularly bad and in the Cyclops almost useless because of the spare wheel stowage position. In addition, the radial tyres commonly used on P4s nowadays for reasons of durability, availability and better handling are of a size (185-15) which will not fit into an unmodified spare wheel tray; consequently, spare wheels usually end up in the boot, thus effectively leaving no luggage space at all!

On the performance side, the 60, 75, 80 and 105R are the least accelerative models, while the 100, 105/105S and 110 are the quickest. Driving pleasure may also be influenced by transmission arrangements. Freewheels were standard until 1955, and continued to be available until 1959 as an alternative to overdrive; synchromesh covered third and top only until 1953, when it was extended to second gear as well. The 105R, of course, had automatic transmission.

As for desirability, the 'Cyclops' probably rates as the most interesting P4, principally because of its rarity, but its odd frontal design is not to everyone's taste. There is no doubt, however, that the best all-round bets are the 100 and 105/105S models.

Moving on now to the P5, there is a choice of two body shapes: Saloon and (after 1962) Coupe. Coupe models have less interior room and were not available as six-seaters, while Saloons were available with a bench front seat until the arrival of Mk III models in 1965 (although Mk II manual transmission Saloons could not be fitted with the bench seat). The Mk III seats are probably the most comfortable and were carried over for the 3.5-litre models in 1967. It was possible on Mk III and later Saloons to specify the optional bench rear seat, which gave the car a seating capacity of five. The V8-engined cars have several cosmetic exterior differences, which may or may not appeal to the individual's taste.

Early cars did not have the front disc brakes introduced in 1960, and there is no doubt that pre-Mk II models without the Weslake-head engine were pretty lethargic, especially the automatics. Later 3-litre automatics are not that much more rapid, and tend also to be fuel guzzlers because of the inefficiencies of the transmission. The type 35 gearbox introduced on Mk III models does not help in this respect, although the altered gearing gives the cars rather more restful high-speed cruising. The best transmission to go for on a 3-litre is the four-speed with overdrive gearbox of Mk II/III models, that of Mk I/IA cars being close to its tolerance limit with the 3-litre engine. The V8-engined cars afford no choice of transmission as all are automatic; they are nevertheless faster and even slightly more economical than the 3-litre. PAS was standardized on all Coupes and then on Saloons after autumn 1964, having been optionally available since 1959. Non-PAS cars, especially those prior to the steering ratio change made with Mk IIb models, have heavy steering.

The rarest P5s are the 2.4-litre and the 2.6-litre variants, although the model generally reckoned to be the most desirable is the 3.5-litre Coupe with its combination of good looks and V8 performance. After that, the best model to go for is a manual-transmission Mk II or Mk III 3-litre with PAS. There are, of course, those who would say that the 3-litre loses much of its luxury-car character without automatic transmission. The individual characteristics of Mk I models gives them an interest value which is heightened by the fact that only small numbers have survived, but they are rather deficient in both performance and handling.

As for the P6, it was always intended as a high-performance saloon and the most sought-after model is therefore the 3500S with the V8 engine and manual transmission. Pre-1970 facelift cars of all kinds are now getting hard to find, and a particular favourite among these is the 2000TC. Estates are also highly prized, and even the 2000 Automatic – a slow, thirsty and rather noisy car – now has its devotees. However, the best all-round cars are probably the post-1970 3500 models with automatic transmission and the final 2200 models, which combine good mid-range torque with refinement and reasonable economy.

Bodyshells did not change over the years, and the major visual differences are between the pre-1970 and the facelifted post-1970 models. Some enthusiasts argue that the extra trim strips, vinyl roofs and quarter-panels, and 'power-bulge' bonnet of the later cars simply detract from the purity of the original styling; others, however, see the facelift as a welcome rejuvenation for cars which looked fat and uninteresting in their original form. The later cars certainly did have much-improved instrumentation (single-carb four-cylinders excepted), however. Seating, for four only, was always leather on the early cars, but Ambla PVC and cloth appeared during the 1970s. Some owners argue fiercely in favour of leather while others welcome the hard-wearing qualities of cloth, but Ambla has few devotees.

Enthusiasts still tend to value the high-performance models of the SD1 above the others, and so the most expensive ones around are late-model Vitesse (especially with the rare twin-plenum injection system) and Vanden Plas EFi types. Even though a model like the V8-S is rare, well-equipped and therefore theoretically desirable, most examples by now are little more than a catalogue of expensive disasters waiting to happen. At the time of writing, few people want a 2000 or 2300 of any kind, while early six-cylinders are unloved and the turbodiesels are very rare indeed (at least in Britain).

Even though the bodyshell of the SD1 remained fundamentally unchanged throughout the car's production run, the visual changes introduced on the 1982 models do serve to polarize enthusiast opinion. The earlier cars certainly do look plainer, and their interiors are much less inviting. Some enthusiasts argue that only the later Vanden Plas cars with their leather upholstery and wood trim recreate the traditional Rover ambience, and this may also be a powerful factor in influencing choice.

**The examination**

Having decided on the model that is wanted, the next stage is to go out and find it. At this point, disappointment and disillusionment are likely to set in, as the cars on offer are usually suffering from a variety of unpleasant maladies (otherwise, why would their owners part with them?). The wise would-be owner of a Classic Rover will inspect a potential purchase with a clear idea of the ills to which the model in question is prone; even better, he will seek the assistance of a fellow-enthusiast who is familiar with the model.

One point that is worth bearing in mind from the outset is that the sumptuous wood-and-leather interiors found on the vast majority of the 1945-86 Rovers can be very expensive to restore. As a poor interior destroys one of the most delightful Rover characteristics, it is worth double-checking that any necessary repairs really are feasible. Although wood can be revarnished, it is not easy to get a finish as good as the original, and the cost of leather repairs puts major restoration of damaged upholstery beyond the means of the average enthusiast.

Going on to consider the model-ranges one by one, it is comforting to report that the 1946-47 cars have a strong chassis, and unless there are signs of severe rusting, accident damage, or the like, this component will probably be sound. Spring shackles do seize, but unless springs have broken in consequence this is not too great a problem. Mechanical brakes are frequently badly adjusted, which can account for odd braking behaviour.

The main enemy of pre-P3 bodies (particularly Tourers) is rot in the timber framing. Reframing is expensive, time-consuming and frustrating, so a car with this sort of problem is best avoided. Chronic wood-rot can often be detected by its smell, and by a general mustiness about the car, while doors which drop when opened are a further indicator of trouble with the body frame. One good way of checking overall structural soundness is to jump (lightly) on the running-boards, although it is not a technique generally appreciated by the seller!

On the mechanical side, the best way to check if all is in order is by a road-test. The 100mm engine does rattle after high mileages as there is no timing chain tensioner to take up the slack in the chain, but this need not cause undue concern unless valve and timing troubles are suspected as well. All gearboxes will whine in first gear, but a rattle when the clutch is depressed will indicate a worn gearbox layshaft. Neglected or blocked Bijur lubrication systems will provoke all kinds of problems unless chassis greasing has been regularly carried out, and it is worth remembering that these systems are troublesome and will often have been disconnected.

The structural side of P3 models presents special problems as there is no chassis behind the rear axle and the rear springs are attached at their rearmost end to a crossmember mounted on the body. The poor quality of much early postwar steel has ensured that rusty rear ends have sealed the fate of many otherwise serviceable cars. On suspect examples, a realistic assessment should be made of whether repairs are economically feasible; after nearly 50 years, major surgery will almost certainly be needed if it has not already been carried out.

The front suspension of a P3 should also be examined closely. Coil springs have been unobtainable for some time and a car which needs extensive work on the IFS may have only scrap value. Engines are not usually problematical, although high-mileage or neglected examples do consume prodigious quantities of oil.

The P3, of course, was the first Rover fitted with the IOE engine, which in various forms powered all P4 models except the 80, as well as the six-cylinder P5s and certain variants of the Land-Rover. P3s had no oil filtration arrangements as standard, although a canister-type external filter was available as a bolt-on extra. When the P4 arrived in 1949, an oil filter became standard, but the Wipac type fitted to the early cars has not been available for many years, and it is prudent to check what, if any, alternative arrangements have been made.

P4s used three basic varieties of the IOE engine: the original P3 type was fitted in the pre-1955 75 (albeit with changed cylinder head, inlet manifold and carburation), a revised 'spread-bore' type powered the 60, 90, later 75 and all 105 models, while the third type – developed from the 3-litre engine with its seven-bearing crankshaft and revised valvegear arrangements – was fitted to 100, 95 and 110 models. Many parts of these engines were shared with contemporary Land-Rover models, and this eases spares availability to some extent. In all cases, a tapping noise from the top end will indicate wear in the cam followers (a simple replacement job); pre-1959 models had pad-type followers which wear more quickly than the later roller-follower type. This should not be confused with the lighter tapping made by maladjusted tappets, however. Oil consumption of IOE engines is quite high at the best of times, and will increase with age, mainly because the rubber O-rings in the inlet valve guides harden and allow lubricant to seep past into the combustion chambers. Blue smoke from the exhaust when the throttle is blipped will warn of this condition. The only other engine used in the P4 was the Land-Rover-derived OHV unit of the 80, which has no particular vices except a tendency to timing chain rattle and carburettor flat spots.

Also worth checking on P4 models is the front suspension. The kingpins are commonly packed with grease by owners instead of lubricated with EP 90 oil and this leads to rapid wear, detectable by steering wander, and sometimes to seizure. Repair costs are high. Rear leaf springs sag in their old age under the sheer weight of the car, but can always be retempered unless actually broken. Manual gearboxes were inherited in their essentials from the prewar models via the P3 and are subject to the same ailments as on the earlier cars. Sticking overdrive solenoids are also fairly common but not serious, and as for the automatic transmission of the 105R, that is fortunately a robust unit which does not normally give trouble.

P4s are not normally put out of commission by rust, because of their immensely strong chassis, although the outriggers which bear the body mountings can corrode badly and jacking points may also be rendered unsafe. On 1960-season and later cars, the rear chassis side-members above the axle are prone to corrosion, which may in extreme cases be compounded by stress; no-one has yet satisfactorily explained the cause of the problem because the chassis is identical to that of pre-1960 models on which this fault is very rarely found! Still underneath the car, a particular weakness is the metal box which protects the handbrake ratchet mechanism; it can corrode right away, leaving the handbrake mechanism to be attacked by road dirt, which will eventually lead to seizure or some other malfunction. Rust, of course, can make an unsightly mess of front wings; on pre-1957 cars the favourite corrosion spot is on the horizontal surface above the wheel, while on later models mud build-up causes rot to break out around the sidelights and indicators. The lower trailing edge of front wings on all P4s is also a weak spot, and rust will commonly be found in addition around the rear wheelarch (particularly the leading edge and under the body finisher trim), on the rear valances and on the spare wheel door and its hinges on post-Cyclops cars. The bottom of the B/C-post is another rust-prone area and, of course, the doors on steel-panelled cars can quickly turn into lacework once rust has taken hold.

Most of the P4's rust problems are cosmetic, but rust is very definitely the main enemy to look for when inspecting the later cars. The P5's biggest weakness is in its rear quarters, where rust will attack the D-posts and the inner members behind the wings. The early signs of this condition are rusty forward edges to the rear wings, and although a car is readily salvageable if the rust has gone no further, there are many on which new wings have been fitted over rust. Remanufactured D-posts are available, but often repairs can be made by inserting new metal. Rust also attacks the P5's sills, and rotted inner sills will weaken the load-bearing structure to a degree which leads MOT testers to refuse a pass certificate; bent or missing jacking points are a sure sign of trouble which has not been fully rectified. Other structural problems are few, although subframe mountings can rust through and make a car unroadworthy. It is probably generally true to say that a car which looks rusty on the outer panels will be even worse underneath.

Rear springs on P5s sag just like those on P4s, and for the same reason. Front suspension ball-joints are expensive to replace if worn, and wear is detectable through steering shimmy. All PAS systems leak a little, but chronic leaks are a sign of expensive trouble. Jerky or seriously leaky automatic transmissions also herald high repair bills, the more so on pre-Mk III cars with the DG transmission, which cannot be removed from the car independently of the engine. Spares for the DG transmission are hard to find. On V8-engined cars, the type 35 transmission was near to the limit of its torque capacity and it is not uncommon for a thoughtless driver to ruin a gearbox within 50,000 miles or so.

The P5's IOE engine and manual gearbox are subject to the same problems as their P4 counterparts, but the V8 engine is a rather different matter. Its two weaknesses are its alloy construction (waterways corrode and this leads to overheating problems unless the maker's instructions with regard to the cooling system are carried out) and its valvegear. Early examples wore rocker shafts very quickly, although by now most will have been rebuilt with the improved type, and sooner or later the valving of the hydraulic tappets inevitably clogs with oil sludge, leading to noisy valvegear. As the tappets are, of course, non-adjustable, they must be replaced, at some expense, although the type introduced in 1976 for the SD1 models can be used and are said to have a longer life. Another common fault is the light knocking caused by camshaft wear, but this can

usually be disregarded. All V8 engines in P5B cars were designed to run on 5-star (100-octane) petrol, which ceased to be available in the late 1970s. Owners have a choice of rebuilding with low-compression pistons (rare), retarding the ignition timing (a compromise), or doing nothing at all (all too common). In the latter case, misfiring will be apparent under load, and even with retarded ignition the engines may consume exhaust valves in short order.

As the P6B's engine and (automatic) gearbox were the same as the P5B's until 1973, the same comments apply. The type 65 automatic gearbox used after that date is rather more durable than its predecessor, but again leaks may warn of trouble; and the lower-compression engines have exactly the same valvegear and corrosion problems as their early counterparts, even though they are happy on 4-star fuel. The OHC engines of the 2000 and 2200 are long-lived units, although timing chain rattle is very common and indicates a need for adjustment, while tuning of the twin-carburettor models is not as easy as it might appear and is in consequence commonly neglected. Oil leaks from the cam cover are not worrying unless serious. All 2000TC models required 5-star petrol like the pre-1974 season V8s, and unless they have been detuned are likely to burn exhaust valves and to misfire.

Early P6 manual gearboxes are rather notchy and often difficult to put into gear. Noise in neutral indicates worn layshaft bearings, which are more common on pre-1969 season cars. Pre-1972 season gear levers may feel sloppy, but this is to be expected and need not cause concern. On 3500S models it is advisable to look out for a gearbox which has been thrashed by an over-enthusiastic owner. Slipping clutches on all models indicate expensive work ahead, as the engine must be removed before a replacement unit is fitted on a 2000/2200 and the gearbox must come out on a 3500S. (It is just possible to do the job *in situ* on a 2000/2200SC, but certainly not on a TC car.) Driveline clonks in all models are common and are often caused by worn universal joints, of which there are two per driveshaft. Early differentials will often leak oil over the rear brake discs and, also at the rear, the De Dion sliding tube is protected by a rubber gaiter which can split and allow road filth to build up and hinder the correct functioning of the sliding joint.

Although it is normal for P6 steering to be on the heavy side, excessively stiff steering may indicate that lubrication of the steering box and idler has been neglected. Power steering systems, of course, leak in exactly the same way as those on P5s. The P6s are especially sensitive to correct wheel alignment and balance and can wear front tyres very quickly; power-steered cars are the worst offenders in this respect. Brakes are not normally troublesome, although the early Dunlop type were prone to sticking pistons, which in extreme cases could lead to broken discs. P6 springs and dampers are relatively soft for a car with such handling/performance potential and such softness need not be an indication of suspension trouble.

The very worst trap to fall into when buying a P6, however, is to go for a car which has had new outer panels put on over a rusty base-unit. At the time of writing, outer panels are still in plentiful supply, and rusty ones are commonly replaced to disguise more serious problems underneath. Rust usually starts at the rear edge of the front wings and the leading edge of the rear wings, and then works inwards. Sills also corrode and their inner surfaces should always be checked (the outer sills are bolt-on panels with no structural function); warning of corrosion may first be seen inside the car underneath the kick-plates. The boot floor will often rot through and render the boot useless, although this is not a structural problem except in the very worst cases. If in doubt about corrosion in a potential P6 purchase it is always wiser to err on the side of safety; it cannot be stressed enough that a P6 rusts even more seriously than a P5 (particularly the earlier cars with their less effective underbody protection), and that a badly-corroded base-unit is so expensive to repair that a car with severe problems here is probably best regarded as a complete write-off.

Although the SD1 models shared the V8 engine with earlier Rovers, almost everything else about them was new. Their V8 engines have the same weaknesses as earlier types, with the additional complication that automatic chokes on later cars can play up. The fuel-injected engines in Vitesse and Vanden Plas EFi models can also suffer when the ECU (Electronic Control Unit or 'black box') develops a fault, and there are one or two other foibles associated with the injection system.

Of the other SD1 engines, the ones to be most wary of are the six-cylinders. The oil feed to the overhead camshaft in these engines can block without warning, causing seizure and demanding expensive repairs to the cylinder head. The four-cylinder O-series engine is reliable enough, but some examples of the VM turbodiesel suffer from persistent head gasket trouble. As for gearboxes, the 77mm five-speed transmission is fairly strong, although abused examples develop layshaft wear and will whine in the intermediates. Gear selection – particularly on early examples – can be difficult when the gearbox is cold, and Rover recommended replacing the gearbox oil with automatic transmission fluid in such cases.

The biggest problems on early SD1s are likely to be the result of poor build quality. Assembly standards did improve with the 1981 models, but it was not until the facelifted 1982 models arrived that quality control was anything like what it should have been. The paint on pre-1981 examples blisters and dulls easily, and corrosion is usually present in the body seams, wheelarch lips and the doors (particularly the rear doors). Poor fit of interior parts, rattles from the doors and loose or broken items of interior trim are further problems on these early cars. Electrical failures are common – the central locking is a favourite on early SD1s – and the greater electrical complication of the later models usually means that there is simply more to go wrong. It was not until the very last cars, built after spring 1984, that the SD1 was largely free of problems when it was new. The difficulties which that poor quality control causes owners today are countless, and are one reason why SD1 prices remain depressed.

Frankly, SD1 ownership demands an infinite love of the car, an equally infinite patience – and a deep pocket. For that reason, the model is disappearing faster than most other saloon cars of its time. One day, good examples – especially of the early cars – are going to be very rare, despite a build total of more than 300,000 over the 10 years of the range's production.

# CHAPTER 10

# Maintaining a Classic Rover

## Clubs, spares and services

When the first edition of this book appeared, it was still possible to buy many parts for these Classic Rovers through the Unipart spares organization. However, times change. The Rover Group today is a very different organization from the Austin-Rover division of British Leyland in the early 1980s, and even SD1 owners come away empty-handed more often than not when they go to a Rover dealership for spares.

One result of this has been that Rover enthusiasts have recognized more than ever the need to band together to give one another assistance, and the Rover clubs of today are stronger than ever before. Anybody who plans to take on one of the cars covered in this book is well advised to join one of the clubs as a first move – even before buying the car. The clubs today are sources of information and support which is simply unobtainable elsewhere, and they also provide the camaraderie which many owners find an essential accompaniment to ownership of any classic car.

A second and very important result of the changes in the parent company has been that a number of specialists have grown up to cater for the Classic Rover owner. Some of these specialists have become affiliated to the Rover Group's Heritage organization as approved suppliers of parts for older Rovers. Others have established their credibility beyond any doubt through years of successful trading, and many of both types have invested large sums of money in the remanufacture of obsolete items which are essential to keep these Classic Rovers on the road. They deserve the support of every enthusiastic owner of one of these cars.

It would be impossible in a book of this size to list every club and every supplier who can be of assistance. However, the addresses provided in this chapter are those of the principal clubs and of the best-known parts specialists: please do not assume that a club or specialist has been excluded from these lists for any sinister reason. Club addresses do change, as these organizations are run by volunteers, and so it is always advisable to check in the classic car magazines for a current contact address before writing – and please do enclose an SAE when writing to club officials! The clubs will, of course, always be an excellent source of information about specialists over and above those listed here.

### The clubs

Rover Sports Register
*(caters for Rovers of all types)*
Cliff Evans
8 Hilary Close
Great Boughton
Chester CH3 5QP

Rover P4 Drivers' Guild
Colin Blowers
32 Arundel Road
Luton
Bedfordshire LU4 8DY

Rover P5 Owners' Club
Geoff Moorshead
13 Glen Avenue
Ashford
Middlesex TW15 2JE

Rover P6 Owners' Club
Steve Evans
PO Box 11
Heanor
Derbyshire DE75 7YG

Rover SD1 Club
PO Box 12
Owlsmoor
Camberley
Surrey GU15 4WZ

**The specialists**

BDG Rover Parts Centre
*(P4, P5, P6 and SD1 spares)*
318-320 Lea Bridge Rd
Leyton
London E10 7LD
(0181-556-5442)

Classic Rover Spares
*(P4, P5 and P6 spares)*
Jon Wadhams
65 Bridgnorth Rd
Wollaston
Stourbridge
West Midlands DY8 3PZ
(01384-393008)
Callers by appointment only

Ely Service
*(P4, P5 and P6 restoration)*
Tom Norman
Lancaster Way
Ely
Cambridgeshire
(01353-662981)

Geoff Kent
*(P2, P3, P4 and P5 spares)*
1 Essex Road
Rushden
Northamptonshire NN10 0LG
(01933-312456)
Callers by appointment only

John Mann
*(P3, P4, P5, P6 and SD1 spares)*
5 Nevis Close
Loundsley Green
Chesterfield
Derbyshire S40 4NS
(01246-271036)

Meteor Spares Service
*(spares for pre-1950 cars)*
5 Holme Lane
Radcliffe Road
Bassingfield
Radcliffe-on-Trent
Nottinghamshire NG12 2LD
(0115-9811222)

MHA (M.H. Annable & Son)
*(P6 restoration)*
Unit 20
Darley Abbey Mills
Derby DE22 1DZ
(01332-346299)

Motorsport of London
 (formerly Roverpart of London)
*(P5 spares)*
Gordon Stacey
173 Whitehorse Lane
Crystal Palace
London SE2 6RB
(0181-653-4790)

Rimmer Bros. Ltd
*(SD1 spares)*
Triumph House
Sleaford Road
Bracebridge Heath
Lincoln LN4 2NA
(01522-568000)

RPS
*(P4, P5, and P6 spares)*
20 Downton Avenue
Streatham
London SW2 3TR
(0181-761-2469)
Callers by appointment only

S & G Walker
*(P6 spares)*
Unit 12
Oyster Place
Dukes Park Industrial Estate
Chelmsford
Essex CM2 6TX
(01245-460214)

Ray Weekley
*(P4, P5 and P6 spares)*
Unit 1
r/o 3 St Agatha's Road
Coventry CV2 4DX
(01203-653274)

# APPENDIX A

# Technical specifications

*(Note: Unless otherwise specified, all dates refer to model-year)*

## 1946-47 (P2) models

### 10hp, produced 1946-47
Construction: Separate chassis and ash-framed body with steel panels.
Engine: 4-cyl, 66.5mm x 100mm, 1,389cc OHV. RAC rating 10.9hp. 6.25:1 CR. 3-bearing crankshaft, single SU carburettor. 48bhp approx.
Transmission: 4-speed gearbox with reverse and freewheel; synchromesh on 3rd and 4th gears only. Gear ratios 3.37:1, 2.04:1, 1.49:1, 1:1. Axle ratio 4.88:1. Top gear 16.4mph/1,000rpm.
Steering, suspension and brakes: Semi-elliptic leaf springs front and rear with hydraulic piston-type dampers. Burman Douglas worm-and-nut steering. Harmonic stabilizer in front bumper. Girling mechanical brakes with 12in drums. 4.75 x 17 tyres on 17in wheels.
Dimensions: Wheelbase 105.5in. Front track 50in. Rear track 51.5in. Length 152in. Width 62in. Height 62.5in. Ground clearance 6.25in. Dry weight 2,800lb approx. Turning circle 37ft.
Body styles available: 6-light Saloon.

### 12hp, produced 1946-47
As 10hp, except:
Engine: 4-cyl, 69mm x 100mm, 1,496cc OHV. RAC rating 11.9hp. 6.25:1 CR. 3-bearing crankshaft, single SU carburettor. 53bhp approx.
Transmission: Top gear 16.6mph/1,000rpm.
Steering, suspension and brakes: Front and rear anti-roll bars. 5.25 x 17 tyres.
Dimensions: Wheelbase 112in. Rear track 54in. Length 169.5in. Height 63in (Saloon), 61in (Sports Saloon). Ground clearance 6.5in. Dry weight 2,912lb approx. Turning circle 39ft.
Body styles available: 6-light Saloon; 4-light Sports Saloon; Tourer (1947 only).

### 14hp, produced 1946-47
As 12hp, except:
Engine: 6-cyl, 63.5mm x 100mm, 1,901cc OHV. RAC rating 14.9hp. 6.5:1 CR. 4-bearing crankshaft, Solex dual downdraught carburettor. Power output never quoted.
Transmission: Axle ratio 5.22:1. Top gear 17.1mph/1,000rpm.
Steering, suspension and brakes: 5.50 x 17 tyres.
Dimensions: Wheelbase 115in. Front track 52in. Length 172.5in. Height 64in (Saloon). Dry weight 3,192lb approx. Turning circle 40ft.
Body styles available: 6-light Saloon; 4-light Sports Saloon.

### 16hp, produced 1946-47
As 14hp, except:
Engine: 6-cyl, 67.5mm x 100mm, 2,147cc OHV. RAC rating 16.9hp. 6.5:1 CR. 4-bearing crankshaft, Solex dual downdraught carburettor. Power output 66bhp approx.
Transmission: Axle ratio 4.7:1. Top gear 17.7mph/1,000rpm

## P3 models

### 60, produced 1948-49
Construction: Separate three-quarter chassis and all-steel body.
Engine: 4-cyl, 69.5mm x 105mm, 1,595cc IOE. 7.1:1 CR. 3-bearing crankshaft,

single Solex downdraught carburettor. 60bhp SAE.
Transmission: 4-speed gearbox with reverse and freewheel; synchromesh on 3rd and 4th gears. Gear ratios 3.37:1, 2.04:1, 1.48:1, 1:1, reverse 2.97:1. Axle ratio 4.7:1. Top gear 17.1mph/1,000rpm (with 17in wheels); 16.7mph/1,000rpm (with 16in wheels).
Steering, suspension and brakes: Independent front suspension with coil springs and anti-roll torsion bar; semi-elliptic rear springs; hydraulic shock absorbers, piston-type at the front and telescopic-type at the rear (telescopic front shock absorbers fitted for 1949). Burman Douglas recirculating-ball steering. Girling hydro-mechanical brakes with 12in drums. 5.25 x 17 tyres on pressed-steel disc wheels (5.75 tyres on 16in wheels optional).
Dimensions: Wheelbase 110.5in. Front track 51.187in. Rear track 54.875in. Length 171.25in. Width 63in. Height 65in (6-light bodies); 62in (4-light bodies). Ground clearance 7.625in. Dry weight 2,968lb approx (6-light bodies); 2,940lb approx (4-light bodies). Turning circle 37ft.

### 75, produced 1948-49
As 60, except:
Engine: 6-cyl, 65.2mm x 105mm, 2,103cc IOE. 7.25:1 CR. 4-bearing crankshaft, Solex dual downdraught carburettor. 72bhp SAE at 4,000rpm.
Transmission: Top gear 17.35mph/1,000rpm (with 17in wheels); 16.7mph/1,000rpm (with optional 16in wheels).
Steering, suspension and brakes: 5.50 x 17 tyres (5.75 tyres on 16in wheels optional).
Dimensions: Ground clearance 7.875in. Dry weight 3,108lb approx (6-light bodies); 3,080lb approx (4-light bodies).

## P4 models

### 60, produced 1954-59
Construction: Separate chassis and all-steel body with aluminium doors, bonnet and boot lid.
Engine: 4-cyl, 77.8mm x 105mm, 1,997cc IOE. 6.73:1 CR (1954-56); 6.92:1 CR (1957-59). 3-bearing crankshaft, single SU carburettor. 60bhp SAE at 4,000rpm. Max torque 101lb/ft SAE at 2,000rpm.
Transmission: 4-speed gearbox with reverse and freewheel (overdrive optional instead of freewheel, (1957-59); synchromesh on 2nd, 3rd and 4th gears. Gear ratios 3.37:1, 2.04:1, 1.37:1, 1:1, reverse 2.97:1, overdrive 0.77:1. Axle ratio 4.3:1 (4.7:1 with overdrive). Top gear 18mph/1,000rpm; overdrive 21.2mph/1,000rpm.
Steering, suspension and brakes: Independent front suspension with coil springs and anti-roll torsion bar; semi-floating rear axle with constant-rate semi-elliptic springs; hydraulic telescopic shock absorbers. Burman recirculating-ball, worm-and-nut steering with variable ratio. Hydraulic brakes with 11in drums. 6.00 x 15 tyres on pressed steel disc wheels with 4.5in rims (6.40 x 15 tyres optional 1959).
Dimensions: Wheelbase 111in. Front track 52in. Rear track 51.5in. Length 178.25in (178.625in, 1959). Width 65.625in. Height 63.75in. Ground clearance 7.125in. Running weight 3,106lb (3,148lb with overdrive). Turning circle 37ft.
Body styles available: Saloon.

### 75, produced 1950-59

As 60, except:

Engine: (1950-54) 6-cyl, 65.2mm x 105mm, 2,103cc IOE. 7.25:1 CR. 4-bearing crankshaft, twin SU carburettors. 75bhp SAE at 4,200rpm. Max torque 111lb/ft SAE at 2,500rpm. (1955-59) 6-cyl, 73.025mm x 88.9mm, 2,230cc IOE. 6.95:1 CR (1955-56); 7.2:1 CR (1957-59). 4-bearing crankshaft, single SU carburettor, 80bhp SAE at 4, 500rpm. Max torque 113lb/ft SAE at 1,750rpm.

Transmission: 1950-53 models have no synchromesh on 2nd gear.

Steering, suspension and brakes: Progressive-rate semi-elliptic rear springs. 1950-52 models have Panhard rod attached to rear axle casing. 1950 models have mechanically-operated rear brakes.

Dimensions: Running weight 3,265lb (1950-54); 3,262lb (1955-59); 3,304lb (with overdrive).

### 80, produced 1960-62

As 75, except:

Engine: 4-cyl, 90.47mm x 88.8mm, 2,286cc OHV. 7:1 CR. 3-bearing crankshaft, single Solex carburettor. 77bhp SAE at 4,250rpm. Max torque 124lb/ft SAE at 2,500rpm.

Transmission: Overdrive gearbox ΄standard; some non-overdrive cars built, 1960. Axle ratio 4.3:1 (with or without overdrive). Top gear 17.8mph/1,000rpm; overdrive 22.8mph/1,000rpm.

Steering, suspension and brakes: Servo-assisted hydraulic brakes with 10.7in diameter discs at front, 11in drums at rear. 6.40 x 15 tyres optional.

Dimensions: Front track 52.5in. Length 178.625in. Running weight 3,204lb (3,246lb with overdrive).

### 90, produced 1954-59

As 75, except:

Engine: 6-cyl, 73.025mm x 105mm, 2,638cc IOE. 6.25:1 CR (1954); 6.73:1 CR (1955); 7.5:1 CR (1956-59). 4-bearing crankshaft, single SU carburettor. 90bhp SAE at 4,500rpm (1954-55); 93bhp at 4,500rpm (1956-59). Max torque 130lb/ft SAE at 1,500rpm (1954-55); 138lb/ft at 1,750rpm (1956-59).

Transmission: Overdrive optional (1956-59); freewheel available (1954-55). Axle ratio 4.3:1 (with or without overdrive); 3.9:1 optional (1955) with freewheel only. Top gear (4.3 axle) 18mph/1,000rpm; overdrive 23.3mph/1,000rpm.

Steering, suspension and brakes: Servo-assisted hydraulic brakes with 11in drums available with optional overdrive only (1955-59).

Dimensions: Running weight 3,200lb (1954-55); 3,245lb (1956-57); 3,276lb (1956-57, with overdrive); 3,267lb (1958-59); 3,309lb (1958-59, with overdrive).

### 95, produced 1963-64

As 80, except:

Construction: Cars built after March 1963 have all-steel panels.

Engine: 6-cyl, 77.8mm x 92.075mm, 2,625cc IOE. 8.8:1 CR (7.8:1 CR optional). 7-bearing crankshaft, single SU carburettor. 102bhp SAE at 4,750rpm (100bhp at 4,750rpm, low-compression models). Max torque 140lb/ft SAE at 1,500rpm (136lb/ft at 1,500rpm, low-compression models).

Transmission: 4-speed and reverse gearbox without freewheel or overdrive. Axle ratio 3.9:1. Top gear 19mph/1,000rpm.

Dimensions: Running weight 3,287lb.

### 100, produced 1960-62

As 95, except:

Engine: 7.8:1 CR. 104bhp SAE at 4,750rpm. Max torque 138lb/ft SAE at 1,500rpm.

Transmission: Overdrive gearbox standard; some non-overdrive cars built (1960). Axle ratio 4.3:1 (with or without overdrive). Top gear 17.8mph/1,000rpm; overdrive 22.8mph/1,000rpm.

Dimensions: Running weight 3,267lb (3,309lb with overdrive).

### 105R, produced 1957-58

As 90, except:

Engine: 8.5:1 CR (7.5:1 optional). Twin SU carburettors. 108bhp SAE at 4,250rpm. Max torque 152lb/ft SAE at 2,500rpm.

Transmission: Roverdrive automatic transmission, consisting of torque convertor, 2-speed synchromesh gearbox with reverse, and automatic overdrive. Gear ratios 1.74:1, 1:1, reverse 2.9:1, overdrive 0.77:1; torque convertor ratio variable between 2.18:1 and 1:1. Axle ratio 4.7:1. Top gear 21.2mph/1,000rpm ( = overdrive).

Steering, suspension and brakes: Servo-assisted hydraulic brakes with 11in drums.

### 105S, produced 1957-58, and 105, produced 1959

As 105R, except:

Transmission: Overdrive gearbox standard; ratios and synchromesh as for 60. Top gear 18mph/1,000rpm; overdrive 23.2mph/1,000rpm.

Steering, suspension and brakes: 6.40 x 15 tyres optional on 105 only.

Dimensions: Length 178.625in (105 only). Running weight 3,382lb (105S); 3,284lb (105).

### 110, produced 1963-64

As 100, except:

Construction: Cars built after March 1963 have all-steel panels.

Engine: 8.8:1 CR (7.8:1 CR optional). 123bhp SAE at 5,000rpm (121bhp at 5,000rpm, low-compression models). Max torque 142lb/ft SAE at 3,000rpm (136lb/ft at 3,000rpm, low-compression models).

Transmission: All cars fitted with overdrive. Top gear 17.5mph/1,000rpm; overdrive 22.7mph/1,000rpm.

Dimensions: Running weight 3,354lb.

## P5 and P5B models

### 3-litre Mk I, produced 1959-61

Construction: All-steel monocoque with separate front subframe.

Engine: 6-cyl, 77.8mm x 105mm, 2,995cc IOE. 8.75:1 CR (7.5:1 optional on export models). 7-bearing crankshaft, single SU carburettor. 115bhp SAE at 4,500rpm. Max torque 164lb/ft SAE at 1,500rpm.

Transmission: 4-speed gearbox with reverse and optional overdrive; synchromesh on 2nd, 3rd and 4th gears. Optional Borg-Warner type DG 3-speed automatic transmission. Gear ratios (manual transmission) 3.37:1, 2.04:1, 1.37:1, 1:1, reverse 2.96:1, overdrive 0.77:1 (Automatic) 2.30:1, 1.43:1, 1:1 reverse 2.0:1. Overdrive standardized with manual transmission on 1961 models. Axle ratio 3.9:1 (4-speed and Automatic models), 4.3:1 (overdrive model). Top gear 20.1mph/1,000rpm (3.9 axle), 18.3mph/1,000rpm (4.3 axle); overdrive 23.5mph/1,000rpm.

Steering, suspension and brakes: Independent front suspension with wishbones, laminated torsion bar springs and anti-roll bar; semi-floating rear axle with progressive-rate semi-elliptic springs; hydraulic telescopic shock absorbers. Burman recirculating-ball variable-ratio steering; Hydrasteer variable-ratio power-assisted steering optional (1961). Servo-assisted hydraulic brakes with 11in drums, 2 trailing shoes at the front; 10.75in discs at the front (1961). 6.70 x 15 tyres (7.10 x 15 optional) on pressed-steel disc wheels with 5in rims.

Dimensions: Wheelbase 110.5in. Front track 55in. Rear track 56in. Length 186.5in. Width 70in. Height 60.25in. Ground clearance 7.875in. Running weight 3,556lb (4-speed); 3,612lb (overdrive); 3,640lb (Automatic).

Body styles available: Saloon.

### 3-litre Mk IA, produced 1962

As Mk I models, except:

Steering, suspension and brakes: 7.10 x 15 tyres no longer offered.

### 3-litre Mk II, produced 1963-66

As Mk IA models, except:
Engine: 8.75:1 CR (overdrive models); 8.0:1 (Automatic). 134bhp SAE at 5,000rpm (overdrive); 129bhp at 4,750rpm (Automatic). Max torque 169lb/ft SAE at 1,750rpm (overdrive); 161lb/ft at 3,000rpm (Automatic).
Transmission: Gear ratios (overdrive models) 3.37:1, 1.88:1, 1.27:1, 1:1, reverse 2.96:1, overdrive 0.77:1. Top gear 18.68mph/1,000rpm (Automatic).
Suspension, steering and brakes: Power-assisted steering standard on Coupe models; standardized on Saloons (1965-66).
Dimensions: Height 59.25in (Saloon); 56.75in (Coupe). Ground clearance 6.625in. Running weight 3,640lb (Saloon, overdrive); 3,654lb (Saloon, Automatic); 3,727lb (Coupe, overdrive); 3,741lb (Coupe, Automatic).
Body styles available: Saloon, Coupe.

### 3-litre Mk III produced 1966-67

As Mk II models, except:
Engine: Both overdrive and Automatic models now have 8.75:1 CR and develop 134bhp SAE at 5,000rpm, 169lb/ft torque at 1,750rpm.
Transmission: Optional Automatic transmission now Borg-Warner type 35 3-speed. Gear ratios (Automatic models) 2.39:1, 1.45:1, 1:1, reverse 2.09:1. Axle ratio (Automatic models) 3.54:1.
Dimensions: Running weight 3,738lb (Saloon, overdrive); 3,693lb (Saloon, Automatic); 3,738lb (Coupe, overdrive); 3,702lb (Coupe, Automatic).

### 3.5-litre produced 1968, and 3½-litre, produced 1969-73

As Mk III 3-litre models, except:
Engine: V8-cyl, 88.9mm x 71.1mm, 3,528cc OHV. 10.5:1 CR. 5-bearing crankshaft, twin SU carburettors. 184bhp SAE at 5,200rpm. Max torque 226lb/ft SAE at 3,000rpm.
Transmission: Automatic only available (Borg-Warner type 35 3-speed). Gear ratios 2.39:1, 1.45:1, 1:1, reverse 2.09:1. Axle ratio 3.54:1. Top gear 21.4mph/1,000rpm.
Steering, suspension and brakes: Chromium plated and painted pressed-steel Rostyle wheels with 5in rims.
Dimensions: Front track 55.312in. Height 60in (Saloon); 58in (Coupe). Running weight 3,498lb (Saloon); 3,479lb (Coupe).

### 2.4-litre, produced 1962 (export only)

As contemporary 3-litre models, except:
Engine: 6-cyl, 77.8mm x 85.7mm, 2,445cc IOE. No further details available.

### 2.6-litre, produced 1962-65 (export only)

As contemporary 3-litre models, except:
Engine: 6-cyl, 77.8mm x 92.075mm, 2,625cc IOE. No further details known, but probably generally similar to P4 110 engine.
Transmission: Gear ratios 3.37:1, 2.04:1, 1.37:1, 1:1, reverse 2.96:1.
Body styles available: Saloon.
No further details available.

## P6 and P6B models

*Note: These specifications are for home market models only.*

### 2000, produced 1964-66, and 2000SC, produced 1967-73

Construction: All-steel base-unit with outer panels and running gear bolted in place. Panels in steel except for aluminium bonnet and boot lid.
Engine: 4-cyl, 85.7mm x 85.7mm, 1,978cc OHC. 9:1 CR. 5-bearing crankshaft, single SU carburettor. 99bhp SAE at 5,000rpm; 89bhp DIN at 5,000rpm. Max torque 121lb/ft SAE at 3,600rpm; 108lb/ft DIN at 2,500rpm.
Transmission: 4-speed all-synchromesh gearbox with reverse. Gear ratios 3.62:1, 2.13:1, 1.39:1, 1:1, reverse 3.43:1. Axle ratio 3.54:1. Top gear 19.5mph/1,000rpm.
Steering, suspension and brakes: Independent front suspension by transverse bottom links and leading upper links acting on coil springs mounted horizontally to the bulkhead; anti-roll bar. Rear suspension by De Dion-type tube incorporating sliding joint, with transverse location by fixed-length drive-shafts and stabilizer rod. Fore-and-aft location by Watt linkages, with coil springs between front links and base-unit. Hydraulic telescopic shock absorbers. Adamant Marles worm-and-roller steering. Servo-assisted Dunlop disc brakes, inboard at rear, with 10.75in discs at front, 10.25in at rear (1964 – May 1966 approx); Girling units with 10.31in front discs and 10.69in rear discs (May 1966 approx – 1973). 165 SR-14 radial-ply tyres on pressed-steel disc wheels with 5in rims.
Dimensions: Wheelbase 103.375in. Front track 53.375in. Rear track 52.5in. Length 178.5in. Width 66in. Height 54.75in. Ground clearance 6.625in. Running weight 2,760lb.

### 2000 Automatic, produced 1967, and 2000SC Automatic, produced 1968-73

As 2000/2000SC, except:
Transmission: Borg-Warner type 35 3-speed automatic transmission. Gear ratios 2.39:1, 1.45:1, 1:1, reverse 2.09:1. Top gear 19.2mph/1,000rpm.
Dimensions: Running weight 2,775lb.

### 2000TC, produced 1967-73

As 2000/2000SC, except:
Engine: 10:1 CR. Twin SU carburettors. 124bhp SAE at 5,500rpm; 109.5bhp DIN at 5,500rpm. Max torque 132lb/ft SAE at 4,000rpm; 124lb/ft DIN at 2,750rpm.
Steering, suspension and brakes: Wire wheels optional (1967-October 1969 approx).
Dimensions: Running weight 2,810lb.

### 2200SC, produced 1974-77

As 2000SC, except:
Engine: 4-cyl, 90.5mm x 85.7mm, 2,205cc OHC. 9.1CR. 5-bearing crankshaft, single SU carburettor. 98bhp DIN at 5,000rpm. Max torque 126lb/ft DIN at 2,500rpm.
Transmission: Top gear 19.7mph/1,000rpm.
Steering, suspension and brakes: Girling 10.36in front discs.
Dimensions: Length 179.31in. Height 55.25in. Ground clearance 6in. Running weight 2,822lb.

### 2200SC Automatic, produced 1974-77

As 2200SC, except:
Transmission: Borg-Warner type 35 3-speed and reverse automatic transmission. Gear ratios 2.39:1, 1.45:1, 1:1, reverse 2.09:1. Top gear 19.7mph/1,000rpm.
Dimensions: Running weight 2,855lb.

### 2200TC, produced 1974-77

As 2200SC, except:
Engine: Twin SU carburettors. 115bhp DIN at 5,000rpm. Max torque 135lb/ft DIN at 3,000rpm.
Dimensions: Length 180.56in. Running weight 2,829lb.

### Three Thousand Five, produced 1968-70, and 3500, produced 1971-76

As 2000SC Automatic, except:
Engine: V8-cyl, 88.9mm x 71.1mm, 3,528cc OHV. 10.5:1 CR (1968-73); 9.25:1 CR (1974-76). 5-bearing crankshaft, twin SU carburettors. 184bhp SAE at 5,200rpm; 144bhp DIN at 5,000rpm (1968-73); 143bhp DIN at 5,000rpm (1974-76). Max torque 226lb/ft SAE at 3,000rpm; 197lb/ft DIN at 2,700rpm (1968-73); 202lb/ft DIN at 2,700rpm (1974-76).

Transmission: Borg-Warner type 65 3-speed automatic transmission (1974-76). Gear ratios 2.39:1, 1.45:1, 1:1, reverse 2.09:1. Axle ratio 3.08:1. Top gear 23.5mph/1,000rpm (1968-73); 24mph/1,000rpm (1974-76).
Steering, suspension and brakes: Burman recirculating-ball, worm-and-nut steering with variable ratio; power assistance optional. Servo-assisted Girling brakes, with 10.82in discs at front, 10.69in at rear. 185 HR-14 radial-ply tyres on 5.5in rims; Dunlop Denovo run-flat tyres on special wheels optionally available with power steering only (1974-76).
Dimensions: Rear track 51.75in. Length 179.75in. Height 55.75in. Ground clearance 7in. Running weight 2,862lb.

### 3500S, produced 1972-76
As 3500, except:
Engine: 150bhp DIN at 5,000rpm (1972-73); 143bhp DIN at 5,000rpm (1974-76). Max torque 204lb/ft DIN at 2,700rpm (1972-73); 202lb/ft DIN at 2,700rpm (1974-76).
Transmission: 4-speed all-synchromesh gearbox with reverse. Gear ratios 3.62:1, 2.13:1, 1.39:1, 1:1, reverse 3.43:1.
Dimensions: Running weight 2,868lb.

## SD1 models

*Note: These specifications are for home market models only.*

### 2000, produced 1982-86
Construction: All-steel monocoque.
Engine: 4-cyl, 84.45mm x 71.1mm, 1,994cc OHC. 9:1 CR. 5-bearing crankshaft. Two SU HIF44 carburettors (1982-84); two SU HIF44E carburettors with electronic mixture control (1985-86). 101bhp at 5,250rpm. Max torque 120lb/ft at 3,250rpm.
Transmission: 5-speed all-synchromesh gearbox, or 3-speed automatic (Borg Warner type 66 on 1982 models); thereafter GM180). Gear ratios (manual) 3.32:1, 2.09:1, 1.40:1, 1:1, 0.79:1, reverse 3.43:1. Axle ratio 3.9:1 (manual), 3.45:1 (automatic). (Borg Warner automatic) 2.39:1, 1.45:1, 1:1, reverse 2.09:1; (GM automatic) 2.40:1, 1.48:1, 1:1, reverse 1.92:1.
Steering, suspension and brakes: Independent front suspension with MacPherson struts, lower links and anti-roll bar. Rear axle with torque tube, trailing arms and Watt linkage, coil springs and telescopic dampers. Rack- and-pinion steering with optional power assistance. Front disc brakes, and rear drum brakes; servo-assistance standard. 175 x 14 radial-ply tyres on steel wheels with 5.5in rims; optional alloy wheels with 6in rims and 195/70 x 14 tyres.
Dimensions: Wheelbase 110.8in. Front and rear tracks 59in. Length 186in. Width 69.8in. Height 53.5in. Ground clearance 5.4in. Unladen weight 3,048lb.

### 2300, produced 1977-86, and 2300S, produced 1981-86
As 2000, except:
Engine: 6-cyl, 81mm x 76mm, 2,350cc OHC. 9.25:1 CR. 4-bearing crankshaft. Two SU HS6 carburettors (1977-81); two SU HIF44 carburettors (1982-84); two SU HIF44E carburettors with electronic mixture control (1985-86). 123bhp at 5,000rpm. Max torque 134lb/ft at 4,000rpm.
Transmission: 4-speed all-synchromesh gearbox (1977-81); 5-speed all-synchromesh gearbox and 3-speed automatic optional (1977-81); 5-speed all-synchromesh gearbox or optional 3-speed automatic (1982-86). Axle ratio 3.45:1.
Dimensions: Length 185in (1976-81); 186in (1982-86). Unladen weight 3,102lb.

### 2400SD Turbo, produced 1982-85
As 2000, except:
Engine: 4-cyl, 92mm x 90mm, 2,393cc OHV indirect-injection diesel with KKK turbocharger. 21:1 CR. 5-bearing crankshaft. 90bhp at 4,000rpm. Max torque 142lb/ft at 2,500rpm.
Transmission: 5-speed all-synchromesh only, with 0.77:1 fifth gear ratio. Axle ratio 3.9:1.
Dimensions: Unladen weight 3,366lb.

### 2600, produced 1977-80; 2600S, produced 1981-86; 2600SE, produced 1982-84; and 2600 Vanden Plas, produced 1985-86
As 2000, except:
Engine: 6-cyl, 81mm x 84mm, 2,597cc OHC. 9.25:1 CR. 4-bearing crankshaft. Two SU HS6 carburettors (1977-81); two SU HIF44 carburettors (1982-84); two SU HIF44E carburettors with electronic mixture control (1985-86). 136bhp at 5,000rpm. Max torque 152lb/ft at 3,750rpm.
Transmission: Automatic standard from May 1984. Axle ratio 3.45:1 (manual), 3.08:1 (automatic).
Steering, suspension and brakes: Rear axle with Boge self-energizing ride-levelling damper struts. Power-assisted rack-and-pinion steering optional (1977-78), then standard (1979-86).
Dimensions: Unladen weight 3,212lb.

### 3500, produced 1977-80; V8-S, produced 1980; 3500SE, produced 1981-86; and 3500 Vanden Plas, produced 1981-86
As 2000, except:
Engine: V8-cyl, 88.9mm x 71.1mm, 3,528cc OHV. 9.35:1 CR. 5-bearing crankshaft. Two SU HIF6 carburettors (1977-81); two Solex 175CDEF carburettors (1982-84); two SU HIF44E carburettors with electronic mixture control (1985-86). 155bhp at 5,250rpm (1977-81); 157bhp at 5,250rpm (1982-86). Max torque 198lb/ft at 2,500rpm.
Transmission: 5-speed all-synchromesh gearbox, or 3-speed automatic; automatic standard from May 1984. Axle ratio 3.08:1.
Steering, suspension and brakes: Rear axle with Boge self-energizing ride-levelling damper struts. Power-assisted rack-and-pinion steering standard. 185 x 14 tyres on steel wheels with 5.5in rims; optional alloy wheels with 6in rims and 195/70 x 14 tyres.
Dimensions: Length 185in (1977-81); 186in (1982-86). Unladen weight 3,214lb.

### Vitesse, produced 1982-86
As 2000, except:
Engine: V8-cyl, 88.9mm x 71.1mm, 3,528cc OHV. 9.75:1 CR. 5-bearing crankshaft. Lucas L-type fuel injection; twin-plenum engine optional 1985-86. 190bhp at 5,280rpm (approx 210bhp for twin-plenum engine). Max torque 220lb/ft at 4,000rpm.
Transmission: 5-speed all-synchromesh gearbox standard; 3-speed automatic option during 1984 calendar-year only. Axle ratio 2.88:1.
Steering, suspension and brakes: Power-assisted rack-and-pinion steering. Ventilated front disc brakes with four-piston calipers. 205/60-15 tyres on cast alloy wheels with 6.5in rims.
Dimensions: Ground clearance 4.4in. Unladen weight 3,280lb.

### Vanden Plas EFi, produced 1985-86
As 2000, except:
Engine: 190bhp fuel-injected Vitesse engine.
Transmission: 3-speed automatic only.
Steering, suspension and brakes: Power-assisted rack-and-pinion steering. Ventilated front disc brakes with four-piston calipers.
Dimensions: Ground clearance 4.4in. Unladen weight 3,258lb.

# APPENDIX B

# Chassis number sequences and production figures

In the period covered by this book, the Rover Company used no fewer than six different chassis numbering systems (the chassis number became known as the commission number on the P5, P6 and SD1 chassisless models).

## 1946-1949 model-years

Seven-digit numbers, preceded on Export models for 1946-49 by an R or L prefix to denote right-hand or left-hand drive.

| First digit indicates model-year | Second digit indicates model | Third digit indicates body type |
|---|---|---|
| 0 = 1940 | 1 = 10hp | 1 = Saloon |
| 6 = 1946 | 2 = 12hp or 60 | 3 = Sports or 4-light Saloon |
| 7 = 1947 | 3 = 14hp | 4 = Drophead Coupe |
| 8 = 1948 | 4 = 16hp or 75 | 5 = Tourer |

The last four digits indicate the serial number, commencing from 0001 in each series for each model-year.

## 1950-1955 model-years

Eight-digit numbers, preceded on Export models for 1950 only by an R or L prefix to denote right-hand or left-hand drive.

| First digit indicates model-year | Second digit indicates model |
|---|---|
| 0 = 1950 | 3 = 60 |
| 1 = 1951 | 4 = 75 |
| etc | 5 = 90 |

| Third digit indicates body type | Fourth digit (except 1950 models) indicates specifications |
|---|---|
| 3 = Saloon | 0 = Home Market |
| 4 = CKD | 3 = LHD Export |
| | 6 = RHD Export |

The last four digits (five on 1950 models) indicate the serial number, commencing from 0001 (or 00001) in each series for each model-year.

## 1956 model-year
Nine-digit numbers.

| First digit indicates type | Second digit indicates model |
|---|---|
| 3 = Car (ie, as distinct from Land-Rover) | 3 = 60 |
| | 4 = 75 |
| | 5 = 90 |

| Third digit indicates specification | Fourth digit indicates model-year |
|---|---|
| 0 = Home Market | 6 = 1956 |
| 3 = LHD Export | |
| 4 = LHD CKD Export | |
| 6 = RHD Export | |
| 7 = RHD CKD Export | |

The last five digits indicate the serial number, commencing from 00001 in each series. Note: 16 1956-season 90 models were built and numbered before the introduction of the new system. These bore chassis numbers 65300001-65300016.

## 1957-1961 model-years
Nine-digit numbers. The first digit in all cases is 6, followed by a pair of digits in the sequence 00 to 54 indicating model and specification. See chassis number lists for full details; several number sequences were allocated but not actually issued. The fourth digit indicates the model-year (7 = 1957, etc) and the last five digits indicate the serial number, commencing from 00001 in each series for each model-year.

## 1962-1977 model-years
Eight-digit numbers, plus suffix letters. The first three digits, in the sequences 400 to 495 and 725 to 869, indicate the model and specification. See chassis number lists for full details; several number sequences were allocated but not actually issued. The last five digits indicate the serial number, commencing from 00001 in each series. The suffix letters indicate design modifications which are of importance in servicing the car. There is no digit to indicate the year of model-year or manufacture.

## SD1 models (1976-1986)
With the SD1 models, Rover introduced standardized VIN (Vehicle identification Number) codes. A typical VIN would be RRWVF3AA000803. The first eight digits identify aspects of the vehicle's build specification, as shown in the table overleaf. The last six digits are its serial number. After October 1981, three additional identifying digits were added to the group which precedes the serial number, and a typical number would be SARRRHWM7CA211361. Serial numbers began with 000001 in 1976; 1981 models began at 155001; 1982 models began at 200001, and Cowley-built vehicles started again at 250001. The last Solihull-built car was 215736 and the last car of all was 345831.

| PREFIX 1 (Oct 81 on) | PREFIX 2 (Oct 81 on) | MODEL RANGE | TRIM LEVEL (Oct 81 on) | BODY TYPE | ENGINE | MODEL (to Sep 81) | STEERING AND GEARBOX | MODEL-YEAR OR VARIANT | ASSEMBLY LOCATION |
|---|---|---|---|---|---|---|---|---|---|
| SA = Rover | R = Austin Rover | RR = SD1 | A = basic | W = Five-door hatchback | B = 2000 | A = 2300 | 1 = RHD 4-speed manual | A = 1976-80 | A = Solihull |
|  |  |  | E = Vitesse |  | E = 2400 Turbo-diesel | F = 3500 | 2 = LHD 4-speed manual | B = 1981 | M = Cowley |
|  |  |  | F = SE<br>H = S<br>M = Vanden Plas |  | K = 2300<br>M = 2600<br>V = 3500 carb | U = 2600 | 3 = RHD Auto<br>4 = LHD Auto<br>7 = RHD 5-speed manual | C = 1982-86 |  |
|  |  |  | X = Police special |  |  | Z = 3500 EFi | 8 = LHD 5-speed manual |  |  |
| *(1976-1981 type)* |  | RR |  | W | V | F | 3 | A | A |
| *(1982-1986 type)*<br>SA | R | RR | H | W | M |  | 7 | C | A |

## SD1 models
### Production totals
No completely accurate production figures for the SD1 have yet been calculated. The figures given below were provided by the British Motor Industry Heritage Trust but should not be considered definitive because they include only some CKD cars. The total production they suggest is 296,169; BMIHT estimates the figure inclusive of CKD to be 303,345, and in 1986 the Rover Press Office provided a figure of 305,139, exclusive of CKD and of a small number of bodyshells built up into competition cars after production had stopped.

| | | | |
|---|---|---|---|
| 2000 | 20,554 | **3500/3500SE/3500** | |
| 2300/2300S | 42,996 | **Vanden Plas** | 107,916 |
| 2400SD Turbo | 10,081 | **V8-S** | 1,040 |
| 2600/2600S/2600SE/ | | **Vitesse** | 3,897 |
| 2600 Vanden Plas | 108,572 | **Vanden Plas EFi** | 1,113 |

**Notes:**  1.  V8-S figures for 1980 are included in the 3500 totals.
2.  According to BMIHT, 14,376 SD1s were built from CKD kits between 1977 and 1983.

## 1946-1947 model-years
### Chassis commencing numbers

| | 10 Sal | 12 Sal | 12 S.Sal | 12 Tr | 14 Sal | 14 S.Sal | 14 DHC | 16 Sal | 16 S.Sal |
|---|---|---|---|---|---|---|---|---|---|
| 1946 | 6110001 | 6210001 | 6230001 | - | 6310001 | 6330001 | - | 6410001 | 6430001 |
| 1947 | 7110001 | 7210001 | 7230001 | 7250001 | 7310001 | 7330001 | - | 7410001 | 7430001 |

**Note**: 1946-season cars were built between December 1945 and December 1946, 1947-season cars between January and December 1947.

### Production totals

| | 10S | 12S | 12SS | 12T | 14S | 14SS | 14D | 16S | 16SS |
|---|---|---|---|---|---|---|---|---|---|
| 1946 | 1,340 | 1,580 | 240 | - | 620 | 235 | - | 875 | 225 |
| 1947 | 1,300 | 2,300 | 520 | 200 | 700 | 150 | - | 2,325 | 725 |

## P3 models
### Chassis commencing numbers

| | 60 6-light | 60 4-light | 75 6-light | 75 4-light | 75 DHC |
|---|---|---|---|---|---|
| 1948 | 8210001 | 8230001 | 8410001 | 8430001 | 8440001 |
| 1949 | 9210001 | 9230001 | 9410001 | 9430001 | - |

Note: 1948-season cars were built during the 1948 calendar year; 1949-season cars between January and August 1949.

### Production totals

| | 60 6-light | 60 4-light | 75 6-light | 75 4-light | 75 DHC |
|---|---|---|---|---|---|
| 1948 | 655 | 304 | 3,441 | 1,720 | 2 |
| 1949 | 256 | 59 | 1,755 | 919 | - |

## P4 models

Chassis commencing numbers

| | Model | Home Market | RHD Export | RHD CKD | LHD Export | LHD CKD |
|---|---|---|---|---|---|---|
| 1950 | 75 | 04300001 | R04300001 | R04600001 | L04300001 | - |
| | -* | 05300001 | - | - | - | - |
| 1951 | 75 | 14300001 | 14330001 | 14360001 | 1463001 | - |
| 1952 | 75 | 24300001 | 24330001 | 24360001 | 24630001 | 24660001 |
| 1953 | 75 | 34300001 | 34330001 | 34360001 | 34630001 | 34660001 |
| 1954 | 60 | 43300001 | 43330001 | 43360001 | 43630001 | - |
| | 75 | 44300001 | 44330001 | 44360001 | 44730001 | - |
| | 90 | 45300001 | 45330001 | 45360001 | 45830001 | - |
| 1955 | 60 | 53300001 | 53330001 | 53360001 | 53630001 | - |
| | 75 | 54300001 | 54330001 | 54360001 | 54730001 | - |
| | 90 | 55300001 | 55330001 | 55360001 | 55830001 | - |
| 1956 | 60 | 330600001 | 333600001 | 334600001 | 336600001 | - |
| | 75 | 340600001 | 343600001 | 344600001 | 346600001 | - |
| | 90 | 65300001 | - | - | - | - |
| | 90 | 350600001 | 353600001 | 354600001 | 356600001 | - |
| 1957 | 60 | 600700001 | 601700001 | 602700001 | 603700001 | - |
| | 75 | 605700001 | 606700001 | 607700001 | 608700001 | - |
| | 90 | 610700001 | 611700001 | 612700001 | 613700001 | - |
| | 105R | 615700001 | 616700001 | - | 618700001 | - |
| | 105S | 620700001 | 621700001 | - | 623700001 | - |
| 1958 | 60 | 600800001 | 601800001 | - | 603800001 | - |
| | 75 | 605800001 | 606800001 | - | 608800001 | - |
| | 90 | 610800001 | 611800001 | 612800001 | 613800001 | - |
| | 105R | 615800001 | 616800001 | - | 618800001 | - |
| | 105S | 620800001 | 621800001 | - | 623800001 | - |
| 1959 | 60 | 600900001 | 601900001 | 602900001 | 603900001 | - |
| | 75 | 605900001 | 606900001 | - | 608900001 | - |
| | 90 | 610900001 | 611900001 | 612900001 | 613900001 | - |
| | 105 | 620900001 | 621900001 | 622900001 | 623900001 | - |
| 1960 | 80 | 645000001 | 646000001 | 647000001 | 648000001 | - |
| | 100 | 650000001 | 651000001 | 652000001 | 653000001 | - |
| 1961 | 80 | 645100001 | 646100001 | 647100001 | 648100001 | - |
| | 100 | 650100001 | 651100001 | 652100001 | 653100001 | - |
| 1961 | 80 | 74500001 | 74600001 | 74700001 | 74800001 | - |
| -62 | 100 | 75000001 | 75100001 | 75200001 | 75300001 | - |
| 1963 | 95 | 76000001 | 76100001 | - | 76300001 | - |
| -64 | 110 | 76500001 | 76600001 | - | 76800001 | - |

*Prototype 2.6-litre cars.

Production totals (see next page)

**Note:** These production figures are taken from the despatch records of the Rover Company, currently held by BL Heritage. They differ from earlier figures based on financial records published by Graham Robson and repeated by the present author in *The Postwar Rover: P4 and P5*. The present figures are based on model-year; the earlier published figures were based on financial year.

| Year | Model | Home Market | RHD Export | RHD CKD | LHD Export | LHD CKD | Model total | Model-year total |
|---|---|---|---|---|---|---|---|---|
| 1950 | 75 | figures for sub-types not available | | | | | 5,220† | |
| | (*) | 30 | - | - | - | - | 30 | 5,250 |
| 1951 | 75 | 3,211 | 4,400 | 126 | 2,542 | - | 10,279† | 10,279 |
| 1952 | 75 | 1,927 | 997 | 54 | 2,718 | 72 | 5,768 | 5,768 |
| 1953 | 75 | 4,742 | 1,068 | 64 | 2,036 | 90 | 8,000 | 8,000 |
| 1954 | 60 | 2,042 | 63 | 44 | 32 | - | 2,181 | |
| | 75 | 2,783 | 524 | 16 | 677 | - | 4,000 | |
| | 90 | 4,163 | 2,090 | 32 | 1,020 | - | 7,305 | 13,486 |
| 1955 | 60 | 1,395 | 68 | 20 | 8 | - | 1,491 | |
| | 75 | 2,963 | 206 | 12 | 454 | - | 3,637 | |
| | 90 | 5,607 | 2,030 | 62 | 581 | - | 8,280 | 13,408 |
| 1956 | 60 | 1,424‡ | 97 | 15 | 65 | - | 1,601 | |
| | 75 | 2,186‡ | 194 | 6 | 354 | - | 2,740 | |
| | 90 | 6,497‡ | 1,920 | 32 | 321 | - | 8,770 | 13,111 |
| 1957 | 60 | 769 | 60 | 2 | 24 | - | 855 | |
| | 75 | 843 | 105 | 2 | 187 | - | 1,137 | |
| | 90 | 2,256 | 1,007 | 8 | 212 | - | 3,493 | |
| | 105R | 1,700 | 121 | - | 81 | - | 1,902 | |
| | 105S | 1,239 | 135 | - | 128 | - | 1,502 | 8,889 |
| 1958 | 60 | 984 (+790) | 93 | - | 28 | - | 1,895 | |
| | 75 | 1,222 | 85 | - | 115 | - | 1,422 | |
| | 90 | 3,081 | 956 | 12 | 138 | - | 4,187 | |
| | 105R | 981 | 410 (+117) | - | 130 | - | 1,638 | |
| | 105S | 1,476 (+1,581) | 245 (+263) | - | 148 | - | 3,713 | 12,855 |
| 1959 | 60 | 1,529 | 78 | 6 | 30 | - | 1,643 | |
| | 75 | 940 | 55 | - | 43 | - | 1,038 | |
| | 90 | 3,168 | 481 | 16 | 203 | - | 3,868 | |
| | 105 | 1,736 | 162 | 14 | 114 | - | 2,026 | 8,575 |
| 1960 | 80 | 2,792 | 222 | 15 | 56 | - | 3,085 | |
| | 100 | 6,251 | 851 | 45 | 558 | - | 7,705 | 10,790 |
| 1961 | 80 | 1,762 | 110 | 12 | 66 | - | 1,950 | |
| | 100 | 3,867 | 434 | 30 | 169 | - | 4,400 | 6,350 |
| 1962 | 80 | 810 | 33 | - | 22 | - | 865 | |
| | 100 | 3,872 | 349 | 6 | 189 | - | 4,416 | 5,281 |
| 1963 | 95 | 2,206 | 165 | - | 42 | - | 2,413 | |
| | 110 | 2,658 | 133 | - | 41 | - | 2,832 | 5,245 |
| 1964 | 95 | 1,091 | 168 | - | 8 | - | 1,267 | |
| | 110 | 1,690 | 76 | - | 22 | - | 1,788 | 3,055 |

Overall total 130.342

**Model totals:**

| Model | Total |
|---|---|
| 60 | 9,666 |
| 75 | 43,241 |
| 80 | 5,900 |
| 90 | 35,903 |
| 95 | 3,680 |
| 100 | 16,521 |
| 105R | 3,540 |
| 105S | 5,215 |
| 105 | 2,026 |
| 110 | 4,620 |

plus 30 2.6-litre prototypes (*)

† 15 1950-51 season chassis were delivered to Wilks, Mackie & Co for conversion to Marauders. All were home market models.

‡ 154 home market cars for 1956 were converted to 1957 specification.

1958 season: Despatch records are incomplete. Production figures quoted are taken from available records; the figure in brackets is a computed figure representing the missing records. The computation has been based on the overall total of 130,342 chassis drawn from financial records, which is believed to be correct.

# P5 models
Commission numbers

| | | Home Market | Export RHD | CKD RHD | Export LHD |
|---|---|---|---|---|---|
| **3-litre Saloon** | | | | | |
| 1959 Mk I | Manual | 625900001 | 626900001 | - | 628900001 |
| | Auto | 630900001 | 631900001 | - | 633900001 |
| 1960 Mk I | Manual | 625000001 | 626000001 | - | 628000001 |
| | Auto | 630000001 | 631000001 | - | 633000001 |
| 1961 Mk I | Manual | 625100001 | 626100001 | 627100001 | 628100001 |
| | Auto | 630100001 | 631100001 | - | 633100001 |
| 1962 Mk IA | Manual | 72500001 | 72600001 | 72700001 | 72800001 |
| | Auto | 73000001 | 73100001 | - | 73300001 |
| 1963 Mk II | Manual | 77000001 | 77100001 | 77200001 | 77300001 |
| -1966 | Auto | 77500001 | 77600001 | 77700001 | 77800001 |
| 1966 Mk III | Manual | 79500001 | 79600001 | - | 79800001 |
| -1967 | Auto | 80000001 | 80100001 | - | 80300001 |
| **3-litre Coupe** | | | | | |
| 1963 Mk II | Manual | 73500001 | 73600001 | - | 73800001 |
| -1966 | Auto | 74000001 | 74100001 | - | 74300001 |
| 1966 Mk III | Manual | 80500001 | 80600001 | - | 80800001 |
| -1967 | Auto | 81000001 | 81100001 | - | 81300001 |
| **2.4-litre Saloon** | | | | | |
| 1962 Mk IA | Manual | - | - | - | 78800001 |
| **2.6-litre Saloon** | | | | | |
| 1962 Mk IA | Manual | - | 75600001 | - | 75800001 |
| 1963 Mk II | Manual | - | 78100001 | - | 78300001 |
| -1966 | | | | | |
| **3.5/3½-litre Saloon** | | | | | |
| 1967-1973 Automatic | | 84000001 | 84100001 | - | 84300001 |
| **3.5/3½-litre Coupe** | | | | | |
| 1967-1973 Automatic | | 84500001 | 84600001 | - | 84800001 |

Production totals

| | Model | Home RHD Manual | Home RHD Auto | Export RHD Manual | Export RHD Auto | Export RHD CKD Manual | Export RHD Auto | Export LHD Manual | Export LHD Auto | Total | Overall total | |
|---|---|---|---|---|---|---|---|---|---|---|---|---|
| 1959 | Saloon | 1,584 | 768 | 305 | 158 | - | - | 186 | 159 | 3,160 | 3,160 | |
| 1960 | Saloon | 3,061 | 2,236 | 971 | 511 | - | - | 368 | 599 | 7,746 | 7,746 | |
| 1961 | Saloon | 1,661 | 1,532 | 376 | 391 | 6 | - | 212 | 166 | 4,344 | 4,344 | (Mk I: 15,250) |
| 1962 | Saloon | 1,612 | 2,245 | 190 | 382 | 306 | - | 399 | 529 | 5,663 | | |
| | 2.4 | - | - | - | - | - | - | 25 | - | 25 | | |
| | 2.6 | - | - | 1 | - | - | - | 24 | - | 25 | 5,713 | (Mk IA: 5,713) |
| 1963 | Saloon | 1,682 | 2,095 | 173 | 447 | 156 | 42 | 362 | 356 | 5,313 | | |
| | Coupe | 237 | 180 | 15 | 18 | - | - | 58 | 38 | 546 | | |
| | 2.6 | - | - | 6 | - | - | - | 43 | - | 49 | 5,908 | |
| 1964 | Saloon | 1,556 | 2,198 | 174 | 332 | 60 | 72 | 204 | 256 | 4,852 | | |
| | Coupe | 951 | 1,250 | 29 | 92 | - | - | 161 | 83 | 2,566 | | |
| | 2.6 | - | - | - | - | - | - | 27 | - | 27 | 7,445 | |
| 1965 | Saloon | 1,473 | 2,509 | 180 | 267 | 36 | 36 | 164 | 159 | 4,824 | | |
| | Coupe | 722 | 1,198 | 20 | 79 | - | - | 85 | 41 | 2,145 | | |
| | 2.6 | - | - | 8 | - | - | - | 22 | - | 30 | 6,999 | |
| 1966 | Saloon | 146 | 297 | 27 | 62 | - | - | 21 | 28 | 581 | | |
| (Mk II) | Coupe | 46 | 142 | 3 | 17 | - | - | 8 | 9 | 225 | 806 | (Mk II: 21,158) |
| (Mk III) | Saloon | 576 | 1,558 | 38 | 101 | - | - | 98 | 136 | 2,507 | | |
| | Coupe | 425 | 1,117 | 7 | 48 | - | - | 65 | 44 | 1,706 | 4,213 | (1966 season: 5,019) |

| | Model | Home RHD Manual | Home RHD Auto | Export RHD Manual | Export RHD Auto | Export RHD CKD Manual | Export RHD Auto | Export LHD Manual | Export LHD Auto | Total | Overall total | |
|---|---|---|---|---|---|---|---|---|---|---|---|---|
| 1967 | Saloon | 247 | 830 | 50 | 144 | - | - | 61 | 80 | 1,412 | | |
| | Coupe | 132 | 520 | 6 | 81 | - | - | 22 | 34 | 795 | 2,207 | (Mk III 6,420) |
| 1968 | Saloon | - | 2,433 | - | 104 | - | - | - | 116 | 2,653 | | |
| (3.5) | Coupe | - | 1,610 | - | 80 | - | - | - | 89 | 1,779 | 4,432 | |
| 1969 | Saloon | - | 2,390 | - | 214 | - | - | - | 118 | 2,722 | | |
| (3½) | Coupe | - | 2,014 | - | 160 | - | - | - | 141 | 2,315 | 5,037 | |
| 1970 | Saloon | - | 1,756 | - | 191 | - | - | - | 120 | 2,067 | | |
| | Coupe | - | 1,320 | - | 128 | - | - | - | 103 | 1,551 | 3,618 | |
| 1971 | Saloon | - | 1,737 | - | 60 | - | - | - | 36 | 1,833 | | |
| | Coupe | - | 1,461 | - | 62 | - | - | - | 26 | 1,549 | 3,382 | |
| 1972 | Saloon | - | 1,290 | - | 70 | - | - | - | 26 | 1,386 | | |
| | Coupe | - | 1,005 | - | 35 | - | - | - | 32 | 1,072 | 2,458 | |
| 1973 | Saloon | - | 735 | - | 84 | - | - | - | 21 | 840 | | |
| | Coupe | - | 785 | - | 37 | - | - | - | 11 | 833 | 1,673 | |

Model totals:  2.4-litre:  25
2.6-litre:  131
3-litre:  48,385 (Saloon 40,402; Coupe 7,983)
3.5/3½-litre: 20,600 (Saloon 11,501; Coupe 9,099)

## P6 models
Commission numbers

| | Home Market | Export RHD | CKD RHD | Export LHD |
|---|---|---|---|---|
| **2000 (1964-1970)** | | | | |
| SC | 40000001 | 40100001 | 40200001 | 40300001 |
| Automatic | 40500001 | 40600001 | 40700001 | 40800001 |
| S | 41000001 | - | | 41300001 |
| TC | 41500001 | 41600001 | 41700001 | 41800001 |
| Auto Federal | - | - | - | 85800001 |
| TC Federal | - | - | - | 85900001 |
| **2000 Mk II (1971-1973)** | | | | |
| SC | 43600001 | 43700001 | - | 43900001 |
| Automatic | 44100001 | 44200001 | 44300001 | 44400001 |
| TC | 44600001 | 44700001 | 44800001 | 44900001 |
| TC Federal | - | - | - | 43500001 |
| **2200 (1974-1977)** | | | | |
| SC | 47100001 | 47200001 | - | 47400001 |
| Automatic | 47600001 | 47700001 | - | 47900001 |
| TC | 49100001 | 49200001 | - | 49400001 |
| TC (Italy) | - | - | - | 86800001 |
| SC (Nigeria) | - | - | - | 86900001 |
| **Three Thousand Five (1968-1970)** | 42500001 | 42600001 | 42700001 | 42800001 |
| **3500S Automatic (1970-1971)** | 43000001 | - | - | 43300001 |
| **3500 Mk II (1971-1976)** | 45100001 | 45200001 | 45300001 | 45400001 |
| **3500S Manual (1972-1976)** | 48100001 | 48200001 | 48300001 | 48400001 |

**Notes**: 1. No records exist to confirm that any 430-series cars were built. However, sightings of such vehicles have been reported. They may possibly have been prototypes converted from 425-series cars.

2. The numbering system was changed in January 1975 when the 868 and 896-series cars were discontinued. New serial number ranges were then allocated to cater for all varieties of a given model (ie, SC, TC etc), and cars were numbered consecutively within these ranges while the type indicator number changed according to specification. 471/472/474-series cars began at 47100882, continuing from where the 471-series had stopped, but the other ranges started anew as follows:

451/452/453/454 at 45127000    481/482/483/484 at 48113000
476/477/479    at 47704000    491/492/494    at 49108000

In addition, 3500 VIP models built in 1976 were given 861-prefix numbers within the 451/452/453/454 sequence.

**Production totals**

No complete and accurate set of production figures for P6 models exists at the time of writing. Although BL Heritage do have the Rover Company's despatch records for P6 and P6B, these, unfortunately, do not provide a full picture because they contain no details of CKD cars prior to January 1975, and there is some suspicion that details of certain other series (eg, 430-series Automatic 3500S cars with right-hand drive) are missing. Rather than provide an incomplete and only partially accurate year-by-year breakdown of production figures, therefore, it seems sensible to give simply the available overall figures. The despatch records show the following:

| 2000 Mk 1 | | 2000 Mk 11 | | 2200 | |
|---|---|---|---|---|---|
| SC | 79,019 | SC | 14,179 | SC | 9,216 |
| Auto | 16,516 | Auto | 10,418 | Auto | 6,126 |
| TC | 50,768 | TC | 31,810 | TC | 16,368 |
| S | 15 | TC Federal | 238 | TC (Italy) | 560 |
| Auto Federal | 940 | | | SC (Nigeria) | 100 |
| TC Federal | 4,987 | | | **Total 4-cylinder cars: 246,260** | |

| Three Thousand Five | 22,290 | 3500S Auto | 2,043 |
|---|---|---|---|
| 3500 Mk II | 37,709 | 3500S Manual | 17,015 |
| | | **Total 8-cylinder cars: 79,057** | |

**Total all models: 325,317**

In addition, the following CKD cars were built:

| 2000 Mk 1 | | 2000 Mk II | | Three Thousand | |
|---|---|---|---|---|---|
| SC | at least 1,985 | Auto | at least 6 | **Five** | at least 205 |
| Auto | at least 246 | TC | at least 30 | **3500S Manual** | at least 838 |

No estimated CKD figures are available for 3500 Mk II models built prior to January 1975. In addition, at least seven 3500S Automatics with right-hand drive are believed to have been built.

When added to the above totals, these figures give:

**4-cylinder cars: at least 248,959**    **8-cylinder cars: at least 80,107**

**Total all models: at least 329,066**

The figure of 327,208 displayed on the last-of-line P6 in December 1976 appears to have been hastily computed on the basis of despatch records. The discrepancy of 1,891 cars between this and the figure of 325,317 quoted above is exactly accounted for by the commission numbers which were allocated but not used.

# APPENDIX C

# How Fast? How economical? How heavy? Performance figures for Classic Rovers

**1946-47 models***

| | P3 models | | | |
|---|---|---|---|---|
| | 14hp Saloon (1,901cc) | 16hp Saloon | 60 | 75 4-light |
| Maximum speed (mph) | 72 | 77.6 | 72 | 75 |
| Acceleration (sec) | | | | |
| 0-50mph | 22.2 | 16.2 | - | 18.2 |
| 0-60mph | 41.3 | - | - | 29.4 |
| Standing ¼-mile (sec) | - | 23.0 | - | - |
| Direct top gear (sec) | | | | |
| 10-30mph | 15.7 | 12.8 | 13.5 | 10.9 |
| 20-40mph | 16.7 | 13.0 | - | 11.9 |
| 30-50mph | 21.4 | 13.6 | - | 13.1 |
| Fuel consumption (mpg) | 22-24 | 19 | 30 approx | 23-28 |
| Weight (lb) | 3,209 | 3,136 | 2,940 | 3,084 |
| Original test published | *Autocar* August 19 1938 | *Motor* June 7 1938 | (*Rover* Company figures) | *Autocar* February 4 1949 |

***Notes**: 1. No detailed road-tests of the 1946-47 models were carried out. The figures for their 1930s' equivalents are therefore provided.
2. Road-tests of the 1930s were not conducted to the same exacting standards as their modern equivalents. These figures should therefore be treated as a rough guide only.

## P4 models

| | 60 (freewheel) | 75 (2,103cc) | 75 (2,230cc; freewheel) | 80 (overdrive) | 90 (freewheel; 3.9 axle) | 90 (freewheel; 4.3 axle) | 90 (overdrive) | 95 | 100 (overdrive) | 105R De Luxe | 105S (overdrive) | 110 (overdrive) |
|---|---|---|---|---|---|---|---|---|---|---|---|---|
| Mean maximum speed (mph) | 77.25 | 82.0 | 85.5 | 85.8 | 83.5 | 80.9 | 91.4 | 94.0 | 92.3 | 93.9 | 95.0 | 100.0 |
| Acceleration (sec) | | | | | | | | | | | | |
| 0-30mph | 5.4 | 6.8 | 6.6 | 7.2 | 5.4 | 5.0 | 5.7 | – | 5.7 | 8.1 | 5.5 | 5.4 |
| 0-40mph | – | – | 10.4 | 9.7 | – | – | 8.9 | – | 8.7 | 12.4 | – | 7.7 |
| 0-50mph | 15.5 | 16.2 | 15.6 | 17.4 | 13.3 | 12.7 | 13.8 | 12.9 | 12.9 | 17.4 | 12.8 | 11.6 |
| 0-60mph | 23.2 | 23.1 | 21.0 | 22.8 | 19.8 | 19.6 | 18.4 | 18.0 | 17.9 | 23.1 | 17.9 | 15.9 |
| 0-70mph | 36.4 | 35.6 | 32.3 | 35.4 | 30.7 | 29.0 | 26.4 | – | 26.0 | 30.7 | 26.75 | – |
| 0-80mph | – | – | – | – | – | – | 38.2 | – | 37.1 | 44.1 | 37.7 | – |
| Standing ¼-mile (sec) | 23.1 | – | 22.5 | 23.4 | 21.6 | 21.4 | 21.1 | – | 21.0 | 24.0 | 20.45 | 20.6 |
| Direct top gear (sec) | | | | | | | | | | | | |
| 10-30mph | 10.8 | 12.7 | 11.2 | – | 10.4 | 9.0 | 9.9 | 11.4 | 9.9 | 5.9* | 9.5 | 8.9 |
| 20-40mph | 11.1 | 12.7 | 12.3 | 11.5 | 10.4 | 9.2 | 9.6 | 11.34 | 9.9 | 7.8* | 9.6 | 9.1 |
| 30-50mph | 11.9 | 13.6 | 13.4 | 12.7 | 11.5 | 10.1 | 10.2 | 12.35 | 9.9 | 9.3* | 9.7 | 9.4 |
| 40-60mph | 14.6 | – | 15.2 | 14.7 | 13.6 | 12.0 | 11.3 | 14.25 | 12.3 | 10.7* | 10.6 | 11.0 |
| 50-70mph | 21.8 | – | 20.1 | 17.8 | 16.8 | 15.7 | 13.6 | 16.38 | 13.2 | 13.4* | 14.5 | – |
| 60-80mph | – | – | – | – | – | – | 18.4 | – | 17.7 | 21.0* | 20.8 | – |
| Overall fuel consumption (mpg) | 28.7 | – | 23.8 | 19.8 | 22.3 | 20.7 | 21.2 | – | 19.5 | 20.1 | 18.5 | 18.4 |
| Typical fuel consumption (mpg) | 24-35 | – | – | 18-26 | 20-26 | 20-24 | – | 18-25 | 17-27 | 23.6 | 18-25 | 24.8 |
| Kerb weight (lb) | 3,024 | 3,198 | 3,192 | 3,304 | 3,196 | 3,196 | 3,248 | 3,287‡ | 3,444 | 3,472 | 3,444 | 3,416 |
| Original test published | Autocar August 20 1954 | Autocar July 14 1950 | Motor January 26 1955 | Autocar December 25 1959 | Autocar March 26 1954 | Autocar March 26 1954 | Motor September 21 1955 | (Rover Company figures) | Autocar August 12 1960 | Motor February 13 1957 | Autocar February 22 1957 | Motor January 30 1963 |

‡ Running weight   * Figures taken in 'Drive' (ie, Intermediate gear) where possible.


## P5 and P5B models

| | 3-Litre Mk I (overdrive) | 3-Litre Mk IA (automatic) | 3-Litre Mk II Saloon (overdrive) | 3-Litre Mk II Saloon (automatic) | 3-Litre Mk II Coupe (overdrive) | 3-Litre Mk II Coupe (automatic) | 3-Litre Mk III Saloon (automatic) | 3-Litre Mk III Coupe (overdrive) | 3.5-Litre Saloon | 3.5-Litre Coupe |
|---|---|---|---|---|---|---|---|---|---|---|
| Mean maximum speed (mph) | 96.4 | 93.6 | 108 | 102 | 108.7 | 102.4 | 101.2 | 107 | 108 | 110 |
| Acceleration (sec) | | | | | | | | | | |
| 0-30mph | 5.0 | 6.2 | 4.5 | 5.9 | 4.8 | 6.5 | 5.6 | 4.9 | 4.8 | 3.8 |
| 0-40mph | 7.5 | 9.8 | 7.3 | 8.4 | 7.3 | 9.8 | 8.1 | 7.2 | 6.6 | 5.5 |
| 0-50mph | 11.7 | 14.3 | 10.1 | 12.5 | 10.3 | 13.4 | 11.4 | 10.7 | 8.9 | 7.8 |
| 0-60mph | 16.2 | 20.2 | 14.5 | 17.1 | 15.0 | 17.7 | 15.8 | 15.0 | 12.4 | 10.7 |
| 0-70mph | 22.7 | 27.9 | 19.0 | 24.1 | 20.4 | 26.0 | 21.4 | 20.3 | 16.3 | 14.6 |
| 0-80mph | 31.5 | 38.5 | 26.4 | 35.0 | 29.0 | 34.5 | 29.2 | 28.4 | 21.8 | 19.7 |
| 0-90mph | 46.8 | – | 33.9 | 54.9 | 39.6 | 47.6 | 45.2 | 42.3 | 31.5 | 27.3 |
| 0-100mph | – | – | – | – | – | – | – | – | 45.0 | 39.3 |
| Standing ¼-mile (sec) | 20.3 | 22.0 | 19.8 | 20.8 | 19.6 | 21.5 | 20.8 | 19.6 | 18.3 | 18.4 |

| | 3-Litre Mk I (overdrive) | 3-Litre Mk IA (automatic) | 3-Litre Mk II Saloon (overdrive) | 3-Litre Mk II Saloon (automatic) | 3-Litre Mk II Coupe (overdrive) | 3-Litre Mk II Coupe (automatic) | 3-Litre Mk III Saloon (automatic) | 3-Litre Mk III Coupe (overdrive) | 3.5-Litre Saloon | 3.5-Litre Coupe |
|---|---|---|---|---|---|---|---|---|---|---|
| **Direct top gear (sec)** | | | | | | | | | | |
| 10-30mph | – | – | 8.8 | – | 9.7 | 4.5* | – | 9.1 | – | 2.9* |
| 20-40mph | 8.8 | – | 8.5 | 11.7 | 9.4 | 5.8* | 5.0* | 9.0 | 6.8 | 3.2* |
| 30-50mph | 9.2 | – | 9.2 | 11.7 | 9.7 | 6.9* | 6.9* | 9.3 | 7.6 | 4.5* |
| 40-60mph | 10.3 | 12.8 | 10.1 | 12.0 | 9.9 | 7.9* | 8.6* | 9.8 | 8.5 | 6.1* |
| 50-70mph | 12.4 | 15.5 | 10.8 | 13.2 | 11.1 | 12.6* | 9.9* | 10.8 | 9.6 | 7.2* |
| 60-80mph | 15.7 | 19.3 | 11.6 | 17.9 | 12.8 | 16.8* | 16.0* | 13.1 | 11.8 | 9.9* |
| 70-90mph | – | 35.6 | 13.4 | 30.6 | 17.4 | 21.6* | 27.8* | 19.4 | 15.5 | 14.2* |
| 80-100mph | – | – | – | – | – | – | – | – | 19.8 | 20.2* |
| **Overall fuel consumption (mpg)** | 19.2 | 17.4 | 17.5 | 15.6 | 17.6 | 15.4 | 17.4 | 18.2 | 19.2 | 17.2 |
| **Typical fuel consumption (mpg)** | 16-24 | 16-25 | 22 | 14-20 | 16-22 | 19.15 | 20.9 | 16-23 | 20 | 22.6 |
| Kerb weight (lb) | 3,640 | 3,730 | 3,752 | 3,780 | 3,752 | 3,780 | 3,765 | 3,836 | 3,517 | 3,517 |
| Original test published | *Autocar* August 21 1959 | *Autocar* December 1 1961 | *Motor* October 3 1962 | *Autocar* November 13 1964 | *Autocar* July 5 1963 | *Motor* March 4 1964 | *Motor* March 19 1966 | *Autocar* May 6 1966 | *Autocar* September 28 1967 | *Motor* October 7 1967 |

*Figures taken using kickdown where possible.

## P6 and P6B models

| | 2000 (pre-production car) | 2000 TC | 2000 Automatic | 2000 SC Mk II | 2000 TC Mk II | 2200 SC | 2200 SC Automatic | 2200 TC | 3500 | 3500 Mk II | 3500 S |
|---|---|---|---|---|---|---|---|---|---|---|---|
| Mean maximum speed (mph) | 104.0 | 108.4 | 94.0 | 98.3 | 105.0 | 100.8 | 101.0 | 108.3‡ | 117.0 | 112.0 | 122.0 |
| **Acceleration (sec)** | | | | | | | | | | | |
| 0-30mph | 4.5 | 3.8 | 6.3 | 4.3 | 3.9 | – | 5.3 | 3.6 | 3.5 | 3.8 | 3.1 |
| 0-40mph | 7.3 | 5.8 | 9.2 | 6.8 | 6.1 | – | 7.6 | 5.7 | 5.1 | 5.7 | 4.8 |
| 0-50mph | 10.1 | 8.5 | 12.8 | 9.7 | 8.6 | 9.09 | 10.4 | 8.2 | 7.0 | 7.9 | 6.9 |
| 0-60mph | 14.6 | 11.9 | 18.0 | 13.6 | 12.2 | 13.42 | 14.5 | 11.5 | 9.5 | 10.8 | 9.1 |
| 0-70mph | 20.1 | 16.5 | 24.7 | 19.5 | 16.5 | – | 20.0 | 15.5 | 13.1 | 14.4 | 12.9 |
| 0-80mph | 27.1 | 22.0 | 35.6 | 27.1 | 22.1 | – | 27.4 | 21.2 | 17.3 | 18.6 | 16.4 |
| 0-90mph | 38.8 | 31.2 | 56.7 | 41.4 | 32.5 | – | 40.0 | 29.4 | 22.9 | 25.4 | 21.2 |
| 0-100mph | – | – | – | – | – | – | – | – | 32.7 | 36.4 | 29.3 |
| Standing ¼-mile (sec) | 19.4 | 18.4 | 21.5 | 19.4 | 18.5 | 19.37 | 19.7 | 18.3 | 17.6 | 17.9 | 16.8 |
| **Direct top gear (sec)** | | | | | | | | | | | |
| 10-30mph | 13.9 | – | – | – | 11.8 | 10.55 | – | – | 3.5* | – | 10.1 |
| 20-40mph | 12.7 | 11.3 | 8.9 | 12.3 | 11.2 | 10.43 | – | 10.0 | 3.7* | – | 8.5 |
| 30-50mph | 11.8 | 10.7 | 11.0 | 12.0 | 11.2 | 11.02 | – | 9.6 | 3.9* | – | 8.1 |
| 40-60mph | 12.6 | 10.6 | 14.3 | 13.2 | 11.2 | 11.55 | – | 9.3 | 5.1* | 8.1 | 7.8 |
| 50-70mph | 15.3 | 12.4 | 18.0 | 15.7 | 12.5 | – | 12.3 | 10.2 | 6.2* | 8.8 | 8.3 |
| 60-80mph | 17.7 | 15.1 | 22.3 | 18.9 | 15.0 | – | 14.4 | 11.6 | 8.5* | 10.8 | 9.0 |
| 70-90mph | 19.6 | 18.1 | 33.3 | 24.4 | 21.4 | – | 19.9 | 15.9 | 11.7* | 14.1 | 10.4 |
| 80-100mph | – | – | – | – | – | – | – | – | 15.5* | 19.1 | 13.5 |
| **Overall fuel consumption (mpg)** | 23.0 | 22.3 | 21.8 | 22.6 | 22.4 | – | 20.5 | 20.4 | 17.5 | 18.0 | 20.1 |
| **Typical fuel consumption (mpg)** | 29.0 | 26.1 | 20-26 | 28.6 | 25.0 | 29.3 | 22.0 | 25.7 | 21.3 | 19.0 | 23.0 |
| Kerb weight (lb) | 2,772 | 2,800 | 2,890 | 2,772 | 2,946 | 2,822 | 2,867 | 2,845 | 2,912 | 2,979 | 2,979 |
| Original test published | *Motor* October 9 1963 | *Motor* October 1 1966 | *Autocar* September 30 1966 | *Motor* December 12 1970 | *Autocar* March 18 1971 | (Rover Company figures) | *Autocar* October 4 1973 | *Motor* October 6 1973 | *Motor* April 20 1968 | *Autocar* October 15 1970 | *Autocar* October 21 1971 |

* Figures taken in D1 range, using kickdown where possible.    ‡ Rover Company official figure.

## SD1 models

| | 2000 5-speed | 2400SD Turbo | 2600 5-speed | 3500 Auto | Vitesse 5-speed |
|---|---|---|---|---|---|
| **Max speed (mph)** | 108.4 | 103.4 | 120.8 | 121 | 133 |
| **Acceleration (sec)** | | | | | |
| 0-30 mph | 4.0 | 4.6 | 3.2 | 3.9 | 2.7 |
| 0-40mph | 6.3 | 6.9 | 4.8 | 5.4 | 4.2 |
| 0-50mph | 8.8 | 10.3 | 6.7 | 7.3 | 5.9 |
| 0-60mph | 12.4 | 14.2 | 9.0 | 9.6 | 7.6 |
| 0-70mph | 16.9 | 21.4 | 12.4 | 12.4 | 10.5 |
| 0-80mph | 23.4 | 29.5 | 15.7 | 15.7 | 13.2 |
| 0-90mph | - | 46.4 | 20.5 | 20.2 | 16.0 |
| 0-100mph | - | - | 27.5 | 27.6 | 20.7 |
| **Standing¼-mile (sec)** | 18.9 | 19.6 | 17.1 | 17.2 | 15.9 |
| **Acceleration in 4th/5th (sec)** | | | | | |
| 10-30mph | - | - / - | - / - | - / - | 9.9 / - |
| 20-40mph | 11.6/19.2 | 10.8/18.2 | 9.0/12.5 | 3.0 (K) | 8.1/12.4 |
| 30-50mph | 11.3/18.7 | 8.0/13.9 | 8.4/11.7 | 3.4 (K) | 7.7/10.9 |
| 40-60mph | 11.4/18.9 | 8.2/12.4 | 8.4/12.2 | 4.2 (K) | 7.5/10.6 |
| 50-70mph | 12.6/20.2 | 12.0/14.6 | 8.4/12.2 | 5.1 (K) | 7.7/12.0 |
| 60-80mph | 14.7/ - | 16.0/18.3 | 8.8/13.0 | 6.1 (K) | 8.2/12.9 |
| 70-90mph | - / - | - / - | 10.0/14.6 | 7.8 (K) | 8.3/13.5 |
| 80-100mph | - / - | - / - | 12.9/ - | 11.9 (K) | 9.2/15.8 |
| **Overall fuel cons'n (mpg)** | 23.3 | 29.6 | 23.3 | 20.6 | 21.8 |
| **Typical fuel cons'n (mpg)** | - | - | - | - | - |
| **Test weight** | 3,269lb (1,483kg) | 3,585lb (1,626kg) | 3,281lb (1,488.5kg) | 3,270lb (1,483.4kg) | 3,508lb (1,593kg) |
| **Original test published** | *Motor* April 3, 1982 | *Motor* Oct 30, 1982 | *Motor* March 24, 1979 | *Motor* Jan 22, 1977 | *Autocar* Feb 12, 1983 |

(K) Figures taken in kickdown.